The Legal Literature of Accounting

On Accounts *by Diego del Castillo*

Translated with an introduction by

PATTI A. MILLS

GARLAND PUBLISHING, INC.

NEW YORK & LONDON 1988

For a list of Garland's publications in accounting, see the final pages of this volume.

Library of Congress Cataloging in Publication Data

Castillo, Diego del.
[Tratado de cuentas. English]
On accounts : the legal literature of accounting / by Diego del Castillo ; translated with an introduction by Patti A. Mills.
p. cm. — (Foundations of accounting)
Translation of: Tratado de cuentas.
Bibliography: p.
ISBN 0-8240-6118-7 (alk. paper)
1. Accounting—Law and legislation—Spain. 2. Accounting—Spain.
I. Title. II. Title: Legal literature of accounting.
III. Series.
KKT923.C3713 1988
346.46'063—dc 19
[344.60663] 88-16309

Design by Renata Gomes

The volumes in this series are printed on acid-free, 250-year-life paper.

Printed in the United States of America

To my parents

CONTENTS

LIST OF ILLUSTRATIONS

PREFACE

It would be difficult in so small a space to acknowledge all of the people who have aided and abetted the creation of this little book, but a few individuals must be mentioned. First, I should like to thank Richard Brief, editor of the Garland Series and Professor of Business Statistics and Accounting at New York University, for his invitation to publish this volume and his continuing interest in my research. I am also greatly indebted to Angelo DiSalvo of the Department of Foreign Languages, Indiana State University, for his painstaking efforts in helping me to smooth some of the rougher edges of the present translation. Over the past year I have enjoyed a lively correspondence with Richard Kagan of the Department of History, The Johns Hopkins University; I found his advice concerning sources and most importantly, how a work of this type is best approached, extremely helpful. My debt of gratitude also extends to Esteban Hernández Esteve of the Bank of Spain, whose own seminal work in Spanish accounting history constitutes most of the foundation upon which the present effort rests. In addition to reviewing the initial proposal for this book, Dr. Hernández Esteve generously provided me with photocopies of the second and third editions of the *Tratado* and of other material which I found difficult to obtain in the United States.

Although this book has benefited in various ways from the efforts of these gentlemen, any deficiencies remaining in it are of course mine alone.

Terre Haute
August 1987

P.A.M.

This volume is an English translation of the sixteenth-century Spanish treatise *Tratado de Cuentas* or *On Accounts* by Diego del Castillo. The broad purpose of the present work is to make this treatise and the issues it raises in accounting history better known. Despite its importance to the field, the *Tratado* has until this point been relatively inaccessible, particularly to scholars in the United States. Original editions of the work are publicly available only in major national libraries;[1] moreover, there is no modern edition of the treatise nor has it previously been translated in its entirety from the Spanish.

For those with an interest in Spanish or early-modern accounting history, the significance of this work is obvious.[2] Despite its preeminence in politics, commerce and culture during the sixteenth century, Spain was poor in terms of an indigenous literature on accounting, making the extant works all the more important. Indeed, the first native text on double-entry accounting -- Solórzano's *Libro de caxa y manuel de cuentas* -- was not published until 1590, some years after Dutch, English, Flemish, French, German and Italian books on the subject had already appeared [Hernández Esteve, 1983, pp. 139-40]. Nevertheless, a few works appeared in Spain anterior to or at about the same time as Solórzano's text, dealing with pre double-entry techniques and other accounting related matters.[3] The earliest known of these is the *Tratado de Cuentas*, first published in 1522.

ACCOUNTING AND THE LAW

Despite its title, the *Tratado* is not a work of accounting literature in a strict sense, but rather a legal treatise with accounting implications. It deserves attention precisely for that reason. Accounting activity has always had social consequences; as a result, accounting practices have been subject to and shaped by legal constraints throughout their history. Accounting historians, however, have largely ignored the important relationship between law and accounting, particularly in the late medieval and early-modern periods where the evolution of double-entry technique remains the dominant concern.

This neglect has produced a distorted view of accounting history, one which reflects the profession's modern preoccupation with business decision making. Historians established long ago that bookkeeping and especially the double-entry system played a notable role in promoting early trade and commerce. The continuing interest in the details of this development, almost to the exclusion of other issues, has produced the impression that in preindustrial society commerce comprised the only area of accounting activity. The historical record tells a different story. Although research in this area is not abundant, there is sufficient evidence to show that accounting activity was of considerable importance in state-building; in the administration of the rapidly expanding judicial system that accompanied the growth of the state; and in regulating the myriad of agential relationships by which late medieval and early-modern society conducted not only its mercantile, but also many of its political, ecclesiastical and familial affairs. Indeed, it may eventually be shown that these other roles, which were essentially legalistic in nature, exerted a greater influence on the development of early Western society than the strictly commercial applications of accounting.

Del Castillo's little book provides a glimpse of this other world. It describes the juridical problems related to stewardship accounting and agential relationships, and the value of account books as legal evidence.

DEL CASTILLO AND HIS TIMES

Del Castillo was a jurist, and as such, was well placed to write on these themes. Other than his choice of profession, little is known about his life.[4] He states in the *Tratado* that he was a "native of Molina," almost certainly Molina de Aragon in the province of Guadalajara, and his other works suggest that he was probably a long-time resident. On the basis of other internal evidence, it is known that by 1522 he was *licenciado* -- possessor of a higher degree in law -- and by 1527 a doctor of law. The date of his death is thought to be around 1551.

In addition to the *Tratado de Cuentas*, Del Castillo wrote at least four other works. His commentary on the Laws of Toro, *Las leyes de Toro glosadas*, first published in 1527, is considered his most distinguished. He was also the author of a manual for confessors; a condemnation of gambling; and an unpublished manuscript on the laws of the *Partidas*. The sixteenth century was not an age of intellectual specialization, and Del Castillo, like other writers of the age, would have felt free to write on a variety of topics.

Writing then occupied at least some part of his time. The *Tratado* provides only a few details concerning the rest of his professional life, but much can be surmised based on what is known of the legal profession in sixteenth-century Spain [Kagan, 1981, pp. 52-78]. Three different kinds of lawyers serviced the Castilian legal system: the advocate or *abogado*; the attorney or *procurador*; and the solicitor or *solicitador*. As a law graduate or *letrado*, Del Castillo would have occupied the highest of these ranks, that of advocate. Legislation required advocates to have at least a baccalaureate degree; many, including Del Castillo, went beyond this requirement and obtained the *licenciado*. As indicated above, Del Castillo was also a doctor of law, a title which at this time was largely honorific and which only a small minority of advocates possessed.

No major study has yet been conducted of the legal profession in early-modern Spain, but it is known that advocates researched cases and devised the legal arguments that formed the basis of their clients' suits. They also prepared briefs and argued cases in court. The royal courts in the major cities provided advocates with their most lucrative source of business. Nevertheless, advocates could also be found plying their trade in smaller provincial centers and villages. A willingness to practice in relatively minor courts may account for Del Castillo's possibly long residence in the town of his birth.

Advocates derived their income from client fees and retainers. Spain in the sixteenth century was an extremely litigious society and advocates as a class enjoyed considerable wealth. Many supplemented the income of their practices by serving as royal commissioners, seigneurial judges and, most importantly for present purposes, estate agents. Although Del Castillo makes no reference to such experience in his treatise, it is conceivable that tenure as an estate agent provided the original inspiration for his text on stewardship.

Regardless of his personal experience, the stewardship function was sufficiently important in early-modern society to have attracted a jurist's scholarly consideration. Land at this time was the principal source of wealth, and the upper aristocracy held most of it. Indeed, this immensely wealthy class, which constituted somewhere around 2 to 3 percent of the population, controlled approximately 97 percent of the land of Castile; in the late fifteenth century they added to their already sizeable holdings large portions of the newly conquered kingdom of Grenada [Elliott, 1963; Lynch, 1964]. In order to administer these vast, oftentimes geographically disparate, tracts it became necessary to delegate oversight of agricultural operations and other kinds of business affairs to various types of managers or agents, called generically *administradores*. These agents were required by law to keep a record of their activities and to communicate this information to their employers or patrons. For this purpose they used accounts and books of accounts.

The particular social, economic and political conditions of the time also created other managerial opportunities, and to believe Del Castillo all such agents were subject to the same kind of reporting requirements as the administrators of agricultural holdings. The Church at this time was a sizeable landholder in its own right and employed agents in much the same way as the secular nobility to oversee the farming and other operations of churches, monasteries and hospitals. Although agriculture remained the principal economic activity, the internal and international trade of Castile expanded considerably during the late fifteenth and sixteenth centuries [Elliott, 1963; Lynch, 1964], and in this area agency relationships developed as well. For example, in cases where several individuals pooled their resources to form a mercantile concern, it was common for them to designate one of their number as a kind of managing partner to handle the company's dealings and trade on behalf of the investment group. As in other agency relationships, this partner was obligated to give an account, in this case to his *companeros*, of what "he received as profit and of what he gave, paid, distributed, used, and of what was lost," in Del Castillo's words. City administrators, collectors of royal taxes, executors of wills and guardians of minor children, among others, labored under similar reporting requirements.

THE LEGAL LITERATURE OF ACCOUNTING

The widespread use of agents to conduct the economic and legal affairs of business, government, church and family made the stewardship function a popular theme in the juridical literature of early-modern Spain. Del Castillo's was the earliest, full-length treatment of the subject. It was followed in 1603 by *De ratiociniis administratorum et aliis variis computationibus tractatus* . . . by Francisco

Muñoz de Escobar, a magistrate of the Chancillería of Valladolid. Written in Latin, *De ratiociniis* was a massive work and is generally regarded as the most complete comment on stewardship accounting from a juridical standpoint. Another work that is normally mentioned in this regard is *Laberintho de commercio terrestre y naval* by Juan de Hevia Bolaño. Published in 1617, the work is actually a treatise on commercial law, indeed, the first and only treatise on Spanish commercial law until the beginning of the nineteenth century. Hevia Bolaño devoted part of his exposition to the legal issues surrounding accounts and account books kept in agency. In addition to these fuller treatments, a number of legal writers touched on the topic in the course of other work.[5]

DEL CASTILLO'S TREATISE

The varied class of deputies, agents, managers -- *administradores* -- and their principals were Del Castillo's intended audience. The purpose of the *Tratado de Cuentas* was to inform, in Del Castillo's words, "tutors, guardians, chamberlains, treasurers and anyone else responsible for administering another's goods" of their legal responsibilities in the area of recordkeeping and reporting. To this end, the treatise is divided into fourteen parts and a prologue addressed to Charles V. In part one the author reviews the various meanings of the terms *cuenta* and *razon* or "account." In parts two through six he discusses who is required to keep and exhibit accounts, to whom the accounts are to be presented, the manner of presentation, and the place and the intervals at which an administrator is in general required to surrender his books for inspection. Part seven treats the proper arrangement of an account book. Part eight discusses how it is that accounts are accepted as proof of the financial realities they purport to represent. After a general discussion of the agent's responsibilities in the ninth section, Del Castillo devotes parts ten, eleven, twelve and thirteen to the procedures to be invoked if errors are detected in the accounts, or if there are outstanding balances. Part fourteen treats the various legal documents that must accompany accounts submitted to the court for probate.

Del Castillo drew heavily for his material on other sources, most of which are squarely in the Roman law tradition. He makes frequent references to Justinian's *Corpus iuris civilis*, the body of the civil or Roman law, and the official to the transaction and any other details likely to lend credence to the agent's records. Del Castillo made the all-inclusive approach a requirement for expenditures but optional for receipts, perhaps under the impression that an agent was more likely to be questioned concerning outflows than inflows.

The text does not describe in detail how a summary of the account was achieved, but the method was probably the same as that employed by Lopez del Campo, Factor General of Spain, later in the century [Hernandez Esteve, 1984, p. 98]. Payments were summed as were receipts, and the totals compared. If receipts exceeded payments, which Del Castillo implies was the normal case, the agent would be indebted to his principal for the balance or *el alcance*. The text expresses this condition as "*[el administrador] fue alcancado.*" If payments exceeded receipts, the principal was the debtor. Any outstanding balance could be carried over to the following period if the agency continued. The first entry -- "the head" -- in the account of a new agency was normally an inventory of the goods and other property committed to the administrator's care.

ADMINISTRADORES AND THE COURTS

The agent's accounts were subject to examination in a court of law. By the sixteenth century an array of local, municipal, ecclesiastical and royal tribunals had grown up to administer Castilian law, and among their functions was the probate of accounts. Del Castillo does not specify at which level of the judicial hierarchy or in which type of tribunal the examination was to be conducted, but he does stipulate that the court of first instance had to possess jurisdiction over the geographical area in which the administration was originally held. In practice, this stipulation would generally not have constituted much of a restriction. Jurisdictions at this time often overlapped, and courts actively competed for cases. Consequently, litigants normally enjoyed a choice of tribunals [Kagan, 1981, pp. 32-33].

In normal circumstances legal opinion required the administrator to exhibit his account book at the end of each year. Reporting periods shorter or longer were also permitted as long as the interval received the agreement of both parties. Whatever the length of the reporting period, theoretically the agent could not be compelled to exhibit his accounts prior to the reporting date unless, as Del

Castillo maintained, he "should make himself suspicious" by dissipating his own goods or worse yet, flagrantly mismanaging those of his principal.

Although protected by law from unscheduled intrusions, the *administrador* still labored under an absolute obligation to present his books for inspection at the customary intervals. Indeed, the *administrador* was obligated to give his patron "all the writings that pertained to the administration," in Del Castillo's words, or face a lawsuit. Under certain circumstances, this responsibility could continue long after the delegation of authority had ostensibly ended. For example, in cases where the agent had not reported at the conclusion of his commission, his obligation to make an accounting remained intact for 30 years, 40 years if he had administered a church or monastery.

Probate of the accounts was conducted by *contadores* who were charged by the court to "do the accounts well and loyally" and "to guard and watch equally the rights of each of the parties without inclination," according to the *Tratado.* In order to assure this impartiality, the investigation was conducted by a committee of auditors named by both parties. If either principal or *administrador* was unable or unwilling to nominate individuals to this panel, the judge was empowered to make such nominations himself.

In his translation of several chapters of *De ratiociniis administratorum*, Jouanique hesitated to use the modern French word for accountant (*comptable*) in place of the original Latin *calculator*, for fear of anachronism [Jouanique, 1965a, p. 19]. There is the same difficulty in rendering *contador* in Del Castillo's treatise. The examination of agential records within the judicial setting appears not to have been a professional calling in the sense of modern accountancy. There were no particular qualifications for the task other than a minimum level of competence; indeed, Muñoz de Escobar claimed that even minors and the infamous could serve as *contadores* [Jouanique, 1966a, p. 39]. Rather, the *contador* served in a temporary capacity at the behest of the parties or of the court, occupying a position similar to that of the executor or the receiver in bankruptcy. Del Castillo relates in part seven of his treatise how he himself served as *contador*, by royal commission, in the examination of a receiver's account.

There is evidence, however, that accounting functionaries, also called *contadores*, were attached in a more permanent way to tribunals at most levels of the judicial hierarchy, in the same manner as magistrates, scribes, constables, porters, receivers and other court officials. It is thought that they bought their offices and were unsalaried, typically for court officials, subsisting on the official fees, bribes and gifts that litigants paid for their services. The particular functions of these court accountants are obscure, but they were involved in some way in producing the permanent written records of court actions required by Castilian law [Kagan, 1981, pp. 37-39]. Whether these accountants were also available to audit agential accounts is unknown.

FORMS OF PROOF AND SUFFICIENT EVIDENCE

At the heart of Del Castillo's treatise is a discussion of the probative requirements the court was to apply in assessing the admissibility and veracity of the agent's record. Such conditions were imposed because legists feared that if book entries were accepted at face value as absolute confirmation of indebtedness, unscrupulous moneylenders would be tempted to create fictitious obligations, making "debtors of whomsoever they wish, by the simple fact of noting down in their books" [Hernández Esteve *et al.*, 1981, VII/2-6].

Central to these requirements was the distinction between confirmatory and supporting evidence. As with modern jurisprudence, in Del Castillo's day not all kinds of proof carried the same weight. Jurists distinguished between those forms that by their existence confirmed the point at law and those that merely lent it support. The capacity to induce "full" or "complete" belief, referred to in the *Tratado* as *plena provanca* or *entera fee*, was inherent in certain types of proof, but in many cases treatment as confirming or supporting evidence depended on circumstances.[8]

In the case of an accounting record submitted as evidence of an agent's honest performance, the contents qualified as confirmatory proof only when it argued against the interests of the book's author. In the case of receivables or other transactions favorable to the author, book entries served merely as supporting evidence, or *semiplena provanca*, which induced only partial belief, *media fe*. According to Del Castillo, this dichotomy reflected the wider legal dictum that a defendant "can testify against himself but not in favor." In order to validate the author's claim against a second party, the evidence of the accounts required the support of additional kinds of proof or *otros indicios*. One common form was the oath sworn by the author on the truthfulness of his record.

The oath as a juridical device entered the Spanish legal tradition from both the Roman and Visigothic law. It developed as a means by which a legal question or suit could be commended to God for resolution in the absence of other compelling evidence. The use of the oath in this manner depended on society's belief in the concept of immanent justice, which accepted the possibility, indeed the probability, of divine intervention in human affairs on a regular basis [Lea, 1974, p. 7]. In the case of the oath, it was thought that divine displeasure at an attempted perjury might be registered, for example, by preventing the swearor from correctly reciting the words of the oath.

By the sixteenth century there was apparently sufficient skepticism regarding the efficacy of the oath among legal circles for Del Castillo to relate arguments against its use as a form of evidence. To the contention that an administrator's oath constituted full proof, Del Castillo responded that according to some sources, "an oath does not make a writing better evidence." It was patently ridiculous, these sources claimed, that "all evidence should depend on one lone man," particularly considering that the testimony of at least two witnesses was required as confirming evidence in other types of legal questions. In his own hierarchy of evidence, Del Castillo was unwilling to grant the oath more than medium weight even when coupling it with evidence of the swearor's good standing (*buena fama*) in the community.

Other forms of proof that Del Castillo cites as reinforcing the evidence of the account book include witnesses to a transaction; a judicial sentence ordering payment of an outstanding balance; a receipt or *carta de pago* prepared by a public notary; and a blameless reputation on the part of the book's author.

In addition to satisfying these general probative requirements, the account book had to be written in proper form in order to compel the court's belief in its contents. If the accounts were unclear, confused or in any way unintelligible, they were presumed fraudulent. Lack of detail in posting transactions could also produce an unfavorable opinion. It was explained previously that Del Castillo did not make use of any particular bookkeeping method a probative requirement although later legal writers did.

It should be noted that important though form was to probative capacity, the air of authenticity it lent a record could be superseded by presumptive evidence. For example, even though correctly entered and ordered, a set of accounts might still fail to induce belief if in the court's opinion the receipts and expenditures they represented appeared unreasonable or improbable. According to Del Castillo, the weight accorded to this presumptive evidence depended on the magnitude of the amounts involved. Small items of expenditure might pass as factual merely on the basis of the court's surmises regarding their reasonableness, even if confusedly written or lacking in detail. Verisimilitude, on the other hand, was but one among several criteria applied to material amounts.

COURT PROCEDURE AND THE AUDIT PROCESS

One of Del Castillo's principal concerns was to present a theory and standards of evidence by which to evaluate agential accounts. Regretably, his description of the actual audit process is less rich, but he does give some idea as to the objectives and procedures of the review. Before going on to a discussion of this process, it should be made clear that examination by the *contadores* comprised only one part of a larger legal proceeding conducted according to Roman law procedure. The purpose of the proceeding, which took the form of a suit, was to settle the account between agent and principal and thus, terminate the agency. In part fourteen of his treatise, Del Castillo discusses the other aspects of the action. These were highly formulaic and common to most civil litigation and consequently, will not be discussed here.

The author makes it clear that the chief responsibility of the *contadores* was the detection of fraud: to "investigate the truth of what is received and justly spent." This assessment was to be based on the information contained in the agent's records and on the opportunity to question both agent and principal in person should the need arise. The auditors were to ascertain, among other items, that receipts and expenditures were recorded in their entirety, and that counts and appraisals had been conducted in an orderly fashion and were neither "too high nor too low." It is at this point that an agent would begin fully to appreciate Del Castillo's earlier admonitions concerning the importance of detailed records. Thrust into the position of having to persuade the court through its *contadores* of the honesty and effectiveness of his administratioin, the agent's chief support was a properly maintained book of accounts. To believe Del Castillo, any administrator whose book was incomplete or contained discrepancies fell automatically under suspicion of fraud.

Should the court determine as a result of this examination that the agent had withheld or diverted goods or revenues unjustly, the administrator was required to make good any shortages of funds. Double damages could also be imposed. For the truly recalcitrant administrator, unable or unwilling to make restitution on demand, Del Castillo recommended incarceration.

Although the detection of fraud and other irregularities constituted the chief focus of the court's concern, plain mismanagement and honest errors if discovered were also to be penalized unless they resulted from circumstances beyond the agent's control. The agent was not entirely without recourse, however. If during the course of the examination errors were discovered in the accounts, the administrator could request that his records be reviewed a second time and another count made. The second examination was to be conducted by two new *contadores*, one named by each party or by the judge should either or both parties demur.

Additional protection was afforded by the segregation of duties within the judicial process. While it was the responsibility of the *contador* to appraise or investigate, only the judge could decide the legal issues and render sentence. Procedure required that the judge subject the accounts to a final review before proceeding to sentence, and the administrator could hope that the judge might catch an item that the accountants had wrongly rejected or misinterpreted. Unfortunately, it was equally as likely that the judge would find against the administrator, observing in Del Castillo's words that "the *contadores* had approved something that they were unable to pass justly."

THE ADMINISTRADOR AS AGENT

Del Castillo makes it plain that the administrator who exceeded the bounds of his authority, either by accident or design, courted financial or other forms of retribution at the time of probate. To help the *administrador* avoid such an outcome, the author outlines in general terms in part nine some of the rights and responsibilities inherent in the agent's office. First, the agent was empowered to disburse funds on the order of either principal or law court, and to the principal's creditors. He was also able to pay himself a salary from the goods and funds he administered, and to receive reimbursement for any expenses he had incurred in the execution of his duties. The administrator was obliged to sell or otherwise transfer the perishable goods in his charge before they spoiled, or indemnify the principal for their loss. He was also required to submit to arbitration any disputes that might arise in the conduct of the principal's affairs. Collection of notes was another common responsibility.

Notwithstanding the large amount of effort the author devotes to haranguing agents on the proper conduct of their duties, and the penalties awaiting them should they err, he concedes that an administrator might suffer financial loss unjustly at the hands of his principal. Such a situation could occur, for example, if the principal failed to reimburse his agent for expenses incurred in the execution of the administration. Armed with the evidence contained in the account book and the opinion of the *contadores*, the administrator could request restitution.

FEATURES OF THE TRANSLATION

The above is only a comment on the treatise's more salient points; for a more complete understanding, the reader is directed to the text itself.

There were three editions of the *Tratado de Cuentas*: Burgos, 1522; Salamanca, 1542; and Salamanca, 1551. The present translation is of the 1551 edition. This edition is approximately 10 folios longer than the previous two, the author having inserted additional material and examples. Although he added material in his last effort, Del Castillo did not introduce substantial changes into the text of the original, which remains the most significant expression of his thought. In the present translation, the material which appears only in the 1551 edition is surrounded by braces.

Del Castillo did not title the individual parts of his tract, but for ease of reference, the sections of the treatise are distinguished here by part number.

Parentheses in the text have been reserved for original parenthetical expressions. Brackets enclose clarifying words or short phrases inserted by the translator. All notes to the text are editorial in nature and are numbered by chapter: they identify people and places; alert interested readers to further works; and in general explain aspects of the text which readers might otherwise misunderstand. Both notes and references appear at the back of the volume and are prepared according to the standard guidelines for research in accounting history.

As a final comment, it should be mentioned that every effort has been expended to make the text as intelligible as possible while preserving some of the flavor of the original language. This was a task easier said than done. As Del Castillo writes in his prologue, he originally composed his tract in Latin, only later rendering it into Castilian. At many points this later version retains the sentence structure of the Latin original which, when combined with the standard difficulties of translating sixteenth-century Spanish, made the present rendering a challenging task.

ON ACCOUNTS BY DIEGO DEL CASTILLO

Treatise on Accounts

by the *licenciado* Diego del Castillo:

native of the city of Molina. In which

appears what an account is and how

tutors and administrators of others' goods

have to render account.

A very necessary and beneficial work:

now added to by the same author.

Prologue

To the very high and mighty lord, King Don Carlos, Emperor Elect,[1] *semper augusto*:

According to both canon law and the laws of these realms, laws ought to be clear and ordered in such a way that all understand them and no one is deceived. Even the prudent misunderstand obscure laws; so much the more will the uneducated and ignorant. And all of us falling into the snare of ignorance, your Majesty as our King and lord, and as maker of the said laws, would be obliged to extricate us from it.

Because the Kings of Spain can make laws, and subjects and local inhabitants must live by them, he who disobeys and goes against them is punished. Making laws obscure and in such a way that they are not understood, would cause many who are innocent to incur penalties. In order to prevent this injury, the most Christian princes, ancestors of your Majesty, ordered the laws that they made in these their kingdoms to be written clearly and in the Castilian language.

And for this reason your Majesty ordered me to turn the tract that I had written in days gone by from Latin into our Castilian language; so that tutors, guardians[2], stewards, treasurers and others that have held in administration another's goods know in what way they must render an account.

Laymen who might have administration of such goods can know from now on how they must account for them.

In this way the work will be universal and all will profit from it so that your Majesty will be served. It will be arranged in such a manner that much of the talk to which the world tends at its cost will cease.

I think it is safe to say that those who might see this work will at least know the ready determination that as a loyal and subject vassal of your Majesty moved me to fulfill your charge; which among wise and prudent men excuses all rebuke. But then we all must fulfill the charge of our King and lord; he who does not comply would merit condemnation.

And thus I the *licenciado*[3] Diego del Castillo, native of the town of Molina,[4] that noble place, and of the title and royal crown of your Majesty, commence the work, having abandoned the talk of those who claim they could also bring it forth and putting first the charge of your Majesty. The work will be verified by the citation of laws and chapters on the margin of each page. Certain doctors will also appear;[5] if anything is well said it may be attributed to them.

And because in the rendering and verifying of accounts there are many different aspects, this treatise will be divided into fourteen parts.

In the first part the meaning of *cuenta* or *razon* [account][6] will be explained.

In the second who is obligated to render one.

In the third to whom it must be rendered.

In the fourth in what way it must be rendered.

In the fifth, when.

In the sixth, where or in what place.

In the seventh, what things are required in the *libro de cuentas* [account book].

In the eighth, what things lend belief to the administrator's book and what do not.

In the ninth, what things administrators can do by reason of their office and what they cannot do.

In the tenth, how if the rendered account is in error, persons review it and count it again and if the error reappears, the first account has to be withdrawn.

In the eleventh, how much time must elapse before a request for another accounting can no longer be made.

In the twelfth, having rendered the account, how payment must be made concerning what it covers.

In the thirteenth, what happens if having rendered the account and made payment, certain items are found in the possession of the administrator or he became rich after he took the office. Is it presumed that he acquired the goods by reason of the office or if not, from where?

In the fourteenth, if the administrator is obligated to give a copy of the accounts and to whom. And in what manner the instrument of the accounts has to be made and when. And in what manner he who requests the account makes the positions. And in what manner the judge will pass sentence regarding the accounts.[7] And whether the sentence which is passed on the accounts can be appealed if the judge orders a recount or payment. Having considered all of which, the account will be settled between the lord and the administrator and any dispute they might have regarding it.

Part One

Here begins the first part.

As for the first part, in which we explain what *cuenta* or *razon* is by relating its various meanings.

First, an account is called a certain and indubitable confirmation. It is called certain and without doubt, because the account that the administrator must give has to be certain and contain no doubt regarding what may be presumed against him.

A motion of the will in those things that can be discerned or known is also called *cuenta* or *razon.*

A confirmed utterance or deed is also called *cuenta* or *razon.*

On the other hand, a movement that originates in the mind through sensate or intellectual means, according to the particular subject matter, is also called *cuenta* or *razon.* It shows or disposes or necessarily concludes the matter as in what is given and received; necessity demands that it be concluded, showing what is received and in what manner expenditure or payment is given.

Similarly, an *cuenta* or *razon* is a movement of the spirit that declares the intent by sight and act; it distinguishes and separates the true from the false.

And these definitions, although certain, apply better and more properly to the *cuenta* and *razon* that witnesses have to give of their utterances, not to the *cuenta* and *razon* that administrators have to give of their office. And because of this I put forward another definition more suitable to our case.

I say that the *cuenta y razon* of the administrator is a memorial of what he gives and receives.

Thus, merchants and persons who have accounts with others write down in one part of their books the receipts and in another part what they dispense. And when they examine their accounts with others, they enter *por data y rescibo.*[1]

Others write down on one page *lo que deve* and on another page *lo que deve de aver*; and when they render account they enter with *deve y deve aver.*

Other accountants make entries *por cargo y descargo*, charging to the administrator all that he receives and accepting from him in discharge all that he gives and spends.

And any of these methods of recording and counting are enough in order to compile an account; but the first two seem better and the last somewhat crude, that is, entering by charge and discharge.

And because above we referred to *cuenta* or *razon*, some would believe that they are different. I say that at law there is no difference between *cuenta* and *razon*. And thus we know what account is.

Part Two

As to the second part in which we relate: who is obligated to render account. I say that if one bequeaths to another in his testament by means of a legacy or inheritance all his goods and stipulates that at a certain time he was to restore them to another, the one who was established first must render an account of the said testator's goods that remained.

Also the tutors and guardians of minors and of their goods, having completed the period of the guardianship, are obliged to render account of the goods that they received and of their fruit, and of what they used and distributed.

Also stewards, receivers, trustees, supply priests, almoners, rectors, treasurers, governors and administrators of the goods of churches, monasteries and hospitals are obliged to render account.

{Where any of these or some cleric were tutor or guardian for the goods of some master or layman, he must render account of the goods he took in administration. Unless he renders an account or if he should render the account badly, he can be taken prisoner, incarcerated and detained until he has satisfied his master for the goods that he administered.

On the basis of certain rights and laws of the realm, canonists says that a secular judge can force a cleric who administers a layman's goods to render an account of them and to seize him unless he does so or if he renders a bad account.

Others say that they would not dare to seize a cleric who had administered a layman's goods without the express license of the pope.

Still others say it is not so simple. If the cleric or ecclesiastic should refuse to render account, or it is presumed that he will flee, in such a case he can be taken prisoner and detained until he renders an account and satisfies the master whose goods he administered, because canonical privilege[1] works only when someone recklessly assaults a cleric and not when the judge seizes him for a just cause. Nevertheless, if the cleric does not have the wherewithal to pay, then he cannot be seized, excommunicated or compelled to cede goods. I hold as true and certain that he cannot be taken prisoner, but recourse can be had against his goods if not against his person.}

Also if two or more persons have a *compañia*[2] and one of them handles the business dealings and trade, he must render account to his partner of what he received as profit and of what he gave, paid, distributed, used, and of what was lost.

Likewise if the mother administered the goods of her children as a guardian or in some other capacity, she must render an account of them, especially those things that are of some quantity. But if they were small in quantity, the mother need not render an account to her children.

But if the mother were married a second or third time, I say that she is obliged to render an account to the children of the first husband of all that come into her hands, even the smallest thing that she received.

Likewise the grandmother is obliged to render account to the grandchildren of the goods that she received from them. Furthermore, the father if he is guardian of the child must give an account of the goods that he received from the child. But if the father should hold the child's goods not as guardian but as legitimate administrator, in such a case the father need not render account of the goods that he received from his child.

{Where the father has emancipated his son[3] or where the son is considered emancipated but lives in his father's house, if the father administers something that he gave to his son on account of marriage, the father must render an account of it to his son and of the fruits and other gains he received from it.

The same will hold in all those cases in which the father has not obtained usufruct[4] of his son's goods, so that administering them, the father will be responsible for rendering an account to his son.

If the father administered the prebend, canonry or dignity of his cleric son, he can be forced by means of an action at law, called *negociorum gestorum*, to give an accounting to his son of all the tithes, fruits and rents that the property may have yielded.

Also, what clerics earn by their own work and industry in ecclesiastical matters, in the service of chapelries or benefices or in other church matters is called *peculio castrense*.[5] And collecting it, the father is obliged to render account, with payment to his son for all of it, except for food and other costs of administration.

The same applies to what the king or other lord should give to the child who is in the power [*patria potestas*] of his father; the property having come into the father's possession, the father must give his son an account of it. Because the usufruct of it does not belong to the father and the son has the same power to dispose of it as with *peculio castrense.*

They say the same about a donation made to a daughter.

And if the son who is in the power of his father or with his mother before marriage should earn something through his work as a soldier with some master or other lord and is not maintained from the goods of his father or mother, he is not obligated to give part of them to his brothers after the death of his father or mother. And if the father or mother receive him at the same time that his brothers have assembled to divide the goods of their father or mother, the brother will draw out first what he earned through such service except where he earned it using the wealth of his father, mother or brothers or been maintained by their wealth as is said.}

Also the executor of the testament or of the last will must render account of what he used or distributed for the soul of the deceased.

Also the older brother who after the death of his father administers the goods of his younger brother must render an account of them.

And where the son, under his father's authority, administered the father's goods while the father lived, the son would be obliged to render an account to his siblings after the father's death. And any salary he has as the manager of the administration is maintained from the father's goods.

And if you would like to know in what things the father is not the legitimate administrator of his child's goods, I say that the goods that the son wins in war and are given him by the troops; and the goods that the lawyer earns by reason of his office and those that some relative or stranger gives to another's child under the condition that the father may not have the usufruct of such goods and of what the child earns. (The child being married, the father does not have usufruct nor is he legitimate administrator of the child's goods.) And should he be guardian of any of these goods or take them under his authority, he would have to render an account of them.

And even where the father might hold usufruct in the child's goods, the father must render an account if he married a second time.

Also if the father should fraudulently distribute or waste the child's goods, he would have to render an account of them.

Likewise, if the father is mad and the child becomes his tutor or guardian of his property, the child would be obliged to render an account of it.

Also the collectors of the royal tributes, tithers, intermediaries, deans and stewards are obliged to render account of the goods and estate that they administered.

Also treasurers, monastic officers in charge of hospitals, receivers, administrators of church seigniories, provosts, collectors and all who administer another's goods must give an account of them.

Also stewards and prelates are obliged to give such an account.

Also he who is named as executor of a testament for pious reasons or from some other cause is obliged to render account of how he expends the goods that were given to him.

{Also, he who takes charge, whether voluntarily or on command, of another's business matters, the *negociorum gestor*, is obliged to render account of the property, litigation and business dealings that he administered or took charge of administering. It is true that the *negociador* [agent] of another's acts does not acquire full authority over them except where the master ratifies what the agent did.

The lord ratifying what was done, the administrator must render account to the lord of all that he gained or acquired in the administration or transaction.

If he concealed anything at the time he rendered account, it is held that he intended to steal it.

It is true that if such a *negociorum gestor* should buy something with the lord's, pupil's or ward's money, he need not give the item that he bought to the master unless he should want the money. But should it be the tutor or guardian that bought the thing with the ward's money, he will be obliged to render the thing that he bought.

The *negociador* can request payment of the useful expenses that he incurred in the master's business matters.}

And generally all administrators of another's goods must render an account of them.

And know that all who administer the goods of others, however they are named, all are called *procuradores* [proxies]; and he is called *procurador* who by order of another administers his affairs, at law or outside of it.

{It is true that all administrators generally are obligated to render account of the goods they administered or of the charge or office they held (as it is said above) except he who has a writing or has proven that he already rendered account; in such a case he need not render it again.

It is considered rendered when it can be proven by a verisimilar and favorable explanation.

But if the account is in error, consider what is said in the twelfth part of the tract.}

And as those who administer the goods of others are obliged to account for them, were they to commit some crime for which the penalty is death, note that death has to be deferred until the administrator has given an account to his master of those goods he administered and of his affairs and lawsuits.

Part Three

As for the third part in which we reveal, to whom the administrator must render the account: I say that the legatee or heir whom the testator ordered to restore some bequest or inheritance, must render account to the one to whom the testator ordered him to make the said restitution.

And the tutor, having finished the period of his guardianship, is obliged to render account to the minor who has attained his majority.

And the judges in these kingdoms according to custom often must appoint a guardian for a minor's goods, the period of the tutelage having finished, and in the legal instrument of the guardianship they empower the guardians to examine the tutor's account for the period that they administered the minors' goods, and this power suffices to examine the account and nothing more.

Likewise, the guardian must render account to his ward who has reached his majority at 25 years of age, and if the minor were to die before he reached this age, the tutor and guardian must give an accounting to his heirs.

The rectors, governors, almoners, proxies, prelates, syndics and other officials of the churches, monasteries and hospitals are obliged to render account of the administration that they held to the bishops, prelates, chapters and convents whom the said prelates authorized to examine the account on their behalf.

{Those who have to examine the account must examine it according to the judgment of a good man.} But know that the guardian by virtue of the power he was given or other persons named by the prelates or governors of the towns, or those who are named by any other particular persons by virtue of the power that was given to them, cannot do more than examine the account and bring it before the judge, prelate or governor so that seen, known and sworn, it may be pronounced as well done. Regarding the closing of the account by the governor or administrator: if for example the guardian or *contador* were to close the guardian's or administrator's account or he were to say that he acquits the guardian because he rendered a good account, e.g., there was no balance due or there was a balance due[1] to the extent of so many *maravedis*[2] and those the guardian paid him. Such a closing would not amount to an end or acquittance of anything. At the very least the minors would be able to ask restitution in entirety. Nor does the tutor prove through such an instrument that he rendered account; the admission or contract he makes to the detriment of his ward does not benefit him; nor the one that the administrator makes to the detriment of the university, monastery or church. It does not injure the principals in anything. If guardians and other administrators could commit such injuries, they would perpetrate large frauds and deceptions on their wards and masters. And law and equity were made more to prevent injuries than to acquire proofs. And if it does not appear that the account was actually rendered, should the minor, reaching his majority, or his heirs ask the guardian for the account again, he would be obliged to render it since it may not be the account that he rendered. And if the guardian or administrator were to say that he wants to prove with witnesses that he rendered the account, it would not suffice, since it does not show if the account was rendered juridically. As will be said more amply in the fourth part of this tract, although the master may wish to allege error in the account, the error could not be proven unless he exhibits the account. And as he who alleges error is obliged to prove it, thus he who says and alleges that he rendered account is obliged to prove by means of the account that he rendered it.

Furthermore, the partner must render account to his copartner.

And the servant or slave must render account to his master.

The administrators of the cities and of other places in the kingdom must render account to the governor, president, *assistente*, or *corregidor*[3] of such city along with *los regidores veynte quatros*[4] or *jurados*[5] of that city. And the reason why the account must be rendered to them is because they represent the whole town and thus the laws of these kingdoms say that the *corregidores* of the cities along with the president or judge who resides in the province can make treasurers and receivers in their province, because they represent the entire town; and for this reason only *los regidores veynte quatros* or *jurados* along with the *assistente*, *corregidor* or governor can enter the town halls.

{If anyone should like to know how someone requests an accounting, he has to develop a libel[6] which requests the accounting. I believe that some say it is enough to put, "I impose a demand against Hulano and I say he was my tutor or guardian, etc. He administered and was obliged to administer my goods; for which reason I ask that he be condemned to render account to me along with any payment." This petition may proceed and is valid without detailing the goods that he administered. They also say that it is valid if it relates a certain sum and in the *processo del pleyto*[7] the items and quantity can be articulated and proven, which has to be requested along with any fruits and damages.}

In short, regarding to whom it is necessary to render account, I say that it must be rendered to all those who claim to have an interest in it.

Part Four

As for the fourth part in which we relate in what manner it is necessary to render account: I say that there are several requirements for a valid account.

The first, that the administrator should exhibit the book that he kept of what he received and spent.

{If he who renders the account is tutor, guardian or some other person obligated to make an inventory of the goods that he receives, he should exhibit this inventory because it is at the head of the account[1]. The inventory and account book are compared.}

The second, that those who examine the account investigate the truth of what was received and justly expended.

The third, that the administrator refund his master for any shortages in the account.

The fourth, to satisfy the lord for all that was badly used or distributed.

The fifth, that the administrator should show that the debtors with whom he contracted had to pay on the date which he contracted with them. So that if the debtors made payment at the date specified in the contract, even though afterwards they should lose their goods or become poor, the risk and loss will be the lord's.

But if the debtor was obliged to pay the debt at a certain term and the administrator permitted so much time to pass after the term that the debtor had opportunity to lose his goods; in such a case the administrator must pay the debt because of his negligence. And if debtors did not have to pay at the time specified in the contract, the administrator must pay the debt to his master, on account of what is said above.

The sixth, the administrator must render an account of those things that he was obliged to do and did not do, as well as of the things that he did do.

I mean that the administrator will be required to indemnify his master if the master had some parcels of wheat and the administrator did not sow them at a suitable time; or having someone who might take them at rent, he refused to let the parcels and they were left in tillage and unrented; or if the master had cattle or sheep and he did not expose them to bulls or rams in their season so that they might multiply and grow; or they were in the habit of grazing until the end of summer or winter and he refused to send them or sent them outside of the customary time; or if there were saltworks and in summer he did not arrange to have the water removed and salt made; or there were vines and he refused to cultivate them, and by not gathering the grapes in time they were lost or in other similar circumstances.

The seventh, it is required that the administrator give to the master all the writings that pertain to him. And if he were to refuse to give them the master can litigate regarding them. And the administrator pays what is adjudged, the quantity having first been appraised and moderated by the judge and the document having been verified.

This is true in the case where the administrator does not want to hand over the writing or he lost it through his own fault; but if it was lost through some mischance or accidentally as through fire or flood or it was stolen along with other of his writings or other possessions, he will not be obliged to pay. Since he was not to blame, he will not incur a penalty.

The eighth, in assigning a valuation to produce that the administrator must pay for because he negligently failed to collect it, there should be consideration of what is a common rent and not what the lord estimates nor what the administrator says.

The ninth, it is required that the account be well rendered and in its entirety and that it should not be given piecemeal, counting one day part of what is received and another day part of what is used; better that all that the administrator received should be counted, without omitting anything.

The tenth, it is necessary that receipts be counted first before the payments, what the administrator received before what he expended.

The eleventh, it is necessary that the account be rendered according to the judgment of a good man.

I mean that in counting as in appraising receipts and expenditures, they are not counted in a disorderly way or at an excessive price or at a low price; but the *contadores* should keep to the middle.

The twelfth, if there are many administrators, all of them should jointly render the account and not each of them on his own behalf. And if one of them were to render the account, it would not be sufficient in as much as the administration was given to all of them. But if each one of them administered in his own behalf, each one must render account of the goods that he administered. And if one has an outstanding balance, another will not be obliged to pay it in as much as the administrators were given the goods separately. But if they were given the goods and the administration jointly, together they have to render the account and each one will be obligated for the administration of the other, because they are known to be obligated one for the other; as it would be with many guardians and proxies to whom a ward's goods are jointly surrendered.

{This article raises an issue which may be difficult to resolve conclusively. It is: a testator leaves two persons as tutors and guardians of the persons and goods of each of his children. As such, the testator leaves them a certain sum; one of them administers the tutelage and renders account of it, the other does not want to or cannot administer it. Is all the bequest owed to the one who administered and rendered account or is something owed to the other? The truth is, the bequest is owed to the one who administered the goods and the other ought not to have anything.

The thirteenth: the administrator must hand over to his master the goods that he received from him which are not justifiably expended and place him in possession of them. And if the administrator should not want to restore them, the lord can seize and imprison him until he should restore them. Although I have not seen this conclusion observed in practice because those who commit private incarceration fear punishment and because a law of this kind has not been tested.}

The fourteenth: it is necessary that if the account is rendered between partners, all that each of the partners lost on account of the *compañia* should be counted or discounted. And it would be the same if on account of his position any other administrator might have lost something not through his own fault.

Likewise, if the guardian or administrator on account of the lawsuits or business affairs of his ward or lord should leave his customary place and incur expenses for food and lodging and other necessary items on his trip, these items have to be taken into account as long as they are moderate in amount.

And because some could ask: Who has to name the persons who examine and verify the accounts, I say that upon petition of the parties the judge can compel the tutor, guardian and any other administrator and the lord to name persons who should examine the accounts, and the parties have to name them. And if any of the parties should not want on their part to name a person the judge can name one on their default; and the nominees have to swear that they will examine the accounts well and faithfully and that they will observe and safeguard equally the right of each of the said parties without inclination.

And upon rendering the accounts and taking this oath, the parties have to be present, which is contrary to the opinions of many who verify accounts for others, who don't permit the parties to be present at the time of the accounting. And this is wrong, because if the *contadores* don't listen to the parties, they cannot well ascertain the truth and the rights of the parties. It is true that in order for the *contadores* to confer upon some items, e.g., whether to approve them as part of the account or not, they can forgo having the parties present. In this case, the *contadores* could not confer nor investigate the truth with the parties present because each of them would speak aloud and oppose what was said against them.

Part Five

As for the fifth part in which we reveal when the administrator must render account. I say that the lord can request the account from the administrator and the partner from his copartner at the end of each year.

{And if two partners held their goods in *compañia* and the division of the goods had occurred a long time ago, the division having been proven, the partner cannot request that the account be redone.

Likewise there are those who invest money in a merchant; they cannot request the account prior to the end of the year of administration. But such a person can request an account of the income from some particular thing or from a special transaction before the said time.

Where someone is obligated to render account within a certain period under pain of some penalty should he not do so; I say that in order to avoid this penalty the administrator can appear before the judge and say that there is a small outstanding balance, which he will specify, and give bond that he promises to pay all which investigation reveals he owes. In this way he will avoid the penalty if he is thought to be short. But if it is certain that he will not be short or there is some doubt, he will not need to render it with the surety, and he will avoid the penalty, should he formally request that the master of the goods he administered examine the account.

Among tutors, guardians or other administrators, the following issue could arise. Someone was decreed tutor, guardian or administrator of a person and his goods. The period of the tutelage or guardianship having finished or the ward having come of age, the ward or his heirs request that an account of the goods that were administered be rendered by means of the inventory that the tutor, guardian or administrator made, which completely proves their intent. The items contained in the inventory once they came into the possession of the tutor, guardian or administrator are presumed to be there still. The tutor, caretaker or administrator responds that 50 or even 60 years had passed since the expiration of the tutelage, guardianship or administration and in all that time never had the ward whose goods were administered or his heirs requested restitution of the goods. Because of this silence over so long a time, it is presumed that the master's right has been satisfied. It is said, too, that the personal action is prescribed after 30 years and prescription of 40 years excludes all legal action, including the account of the administration.

Also they say that the passage of so much time induces total truth.

By the silence of so much time, the master is considered to have tacitly renounced the right to the goods requested by him or his heirs.

They say, too, that in all this time neither the master nor his heirs ever brought suit regarding this matter and therefore, it was demonstrated that the administrator need not render account.

And he who is free or freed by the passage of time is similar to the one who actually satisfied the obligation or paid; and they say he is free after 30 years from action regarding the tutelage.

It is also seen to alienate the one who suffers or who agrees to prescribe against himself.

If anyone should say that the heirs of the tutor or administrator or the tutor himself were in the wrong wanting to prescribe the inventoried goods and because of this wrong could not prescribe; to this he responds that when we treat or speak about the prescription of personal property, what is said to the contrary does not apply, because it applies in the prescription of real estate. Also the children and heirs of the tutor or administrator say that they were able to prescribe the goods contained in the inventory based on the opinions of other doctors, canonists as well as legists. If the lord or his heirs did not request an account from the tutor, administrator or from their heirs, the obligation ends. If the lord owed the tutor a large sum of maravedis and he was not asked to compensate the tutor, in such a case compensation is presumed since between them it was never opposed as was required. Therefore, the tutor or administrator and their heirs remained the lord's debtors, he having against them a public instrument and thus the compensation and not the original prescription applies. To this argument one can respond that if the lord did not ask the tutor or his heirs for the debt they owed him nor did the tutor, administrator or their heirs request from the lord the goods they took as inventory, it does not follow on account of this that the lord or debtor may not be indebted for the contents of the instrument. The debt does not weaken the prescription which is alleged against the lord, but the fact that the one who is prescribed may be a debtor of the one who prescribes hinders the prescription; therefore, the prescription does not apply. Nevertheless, I have not found it written that such an exception can be offered at law and since it cannot be found that such an exception can be offered, we are obliged to follow the rule that says the prescription of longstanding excludes all action, as is said above.

A second prescription: with the inventoried goods restored after so much time had passed in silence, and writings having been made of the account and payment, what if the writings were lost? If it were proven that in the meantime the place where the goods were administered or the tutor or administrator lived had been sacked, or the administrator's house was robbed or burned, the administrator's oath is sufficient to prove that the writing was indeed taken away or burned.

Whence it is said the rout or conflagration having been proven, the existence of the writings or inventory is proven by conjecture. There is also a third reason which supports the presumption that the tutor or administrator had rendered account and paid what was contained in the inventory -- the master of the inventoried goods or his heirs took or saw the inventory a few times or they discussed it with the tutor, administrator or their heirs or with some other person so that the lord or his heirs knew or took note that the tutor or administrator had some goods in administration. Thus it is assumed that he who holds some writing or has seen it knows or knew what it contained or contains.

Furthermore, consideration has to be had if between the lord and the administrator and between their heirs there is a high degree of kinship or blood relationship, because then three things come together: the first, long duration; the second, the combination of relationships; the third, that between them there were transactions and accounts regarding other issues. Inasmuch as what was contained in the said inventory or administration was not retained, it would be completely proven that the tutor or administrator had paid what was contained in the inventory. If, for example, the two things above, namely the passage of time and the combination of relationships, were proven, it would not be sufficient to free the tutor or administrator against what is said; this is the conclusion of many doctors. But the truth is that the passage of so much time is held to replace the rendered account, according to what is said. If with this it is proven that the lord or the lord being deceased, one of his children or heirs, was tutor or held in administration the goods of their tutor, administrator or of his children, it is presumed that the goods contained in the inventory of the first tutor or administrator came into the possession of this tutor or administrator. Then he could pay and satisfy the obligation by means of his own authority without the authority of a judge as it is said in the ninth part of this tract.

If anyone says that this second individual who held the goods of his tutor or administrator in his possession did not want to be paid from those goods so that he could request the goods of the inventory afterwards; to this can be answered that this second person who held the goods of his tutor or administrator in his possession was poor and that while in need no one is presumed to be generous.

It is presumed and considered at law as almost certain that if the administrator is a creditor of the one whose goods he administers, he will be paid for all that is owed him.

Another reason that the master of the goods contained in the inventory was paid from the goods that he afterwards administered for his tutor or the tutor's heirs: that he would do what other diligent administrators would do; if he acted in some other manner, it could be said he was at fault. But guilt is not presumed if it is not proven because guilt has to be proven by him who alleges it; any person, inasmuch as experience, who is a teacher, teaches us.

The administrator holds the goods of his debtor from which, as is said, he can be paid. If it is believed that he is paid from them, he would not be obliged to restore more than what might remain from the goods of his tutor, the tutor's children or heirs that he afterwards administered or had in his possession.

Another condition can occur whereby the goods of the inventory were presumed restored, proving that the master of the inventoried goods or his heirs were very diligent in recovering the goods and the debts owed them and that in that jurisdiction and kingdom justice was done. Another presumption that the master of the inventoried goods has been paid occurs if a minor, come of age, did not have sufficient goods remaining with which to deal or trade; and he entered a *compañia* with another and put into it a great deal of money or he paid a great quantity of debts that his father owed at the time of his death; and some personal property, real estate or livestock from among the contents of the inventory are found in his possession. If he is paid in part from the contents of the inventory when he could be paid in full, it is presumed that the master and his heirs were paid in full. Just as we say that accepting the part is considered the same as accepting the total. This is injurious to the lord's interests. It is true that if someone paid part of what he owed, he is not considered to have paid in full on this basis alone and the creditor could request the remainder owed to him. Since the master and his children in all this time did not sue the tutor, guardian, administrator or their children or heirs regarding the goods contained in the inventory, and there was an especially large quantity of goods, it is argued that they were paid. By making the request, after so much time has past, they demonstrate their injustice. The law presumes that he who shuns judgment distrusts the outcome. To this proposition and the determination of our question some doctors bring the above arguments.

Furthermore, it can be conjectured that the goods of the inventory were restored because the tutor or administrator lent to the master some amount of money, as it appears in a public instrument, without taking security or a bondsman and no mention was made of the goods contained in the inventory being of much greater value. So that it has to be considered a thing so old that it exceeds a 30 or even 40-year period. On account of the signs and conjectures that are named above which, it is said, induce complete proof, it follows that neither the first master of the inventoried goods nor his heirs can request the goods again. Elsewhere it is said that proof made by signs and conjectures is clearly manifest proof.

That which is shown by conjecture is said to be clear. If these presumptions concerned an act that was perhaps not so old, according to some opinions they would not suffice but with an old deed they say insufficient presumptions are enough. It is called an old act when it happened 30 or 40 years ago.

On the basis of these presumptions, inferred by law and man, a definitive sentence in a civil cause can be given. On the other hand, there is a great contradiction or obstacle opposing this: how can presumptions, signs or conjectures constitute proof against a written inventory when the contrary cannot be proven unless by another such writing which says these goods were paid for or surrendered?

Generally, when the debt is proven by writing, the payment, as is said, has to be proven by writing or by five witnesses.

But against this many maintain the contrary, saying that if a writing of the debt is made along with a pact or convention of the parties which has to be proven with another such writing, the payment has to be proven with a writing as is said; but if it is a writing required by law it can be proven indirectly by witnesses. In the same way that they should say or testify that he paid, likewise we say regarding an emphyteutic contract[1] that requires a writing. Payment of the *censo*[2] can be proven with witnesses and thus they infer that against the written inventory the restitution of the goods can be proven not only by writing but with witnesses and presumptions.

Where the tutor or his children and heirs in the meantime sued the lord or his heirs for the money that by contract the lord owed them, and the lord or his heirs countered by requesting that the tutor or administrator restore the goods contained in the inventory, it has to be determined if they countered before the 30 or 40-year period that we spoke of above had expired because in such a case the prescription would be interrupted. But if within the period nothing was said or asked regarding the contents of the said inventory, neither the lord nor his heirs can request it on account of the causes and reasons already given and the law which speaks expressly in this case.

Together with this and other very evident reasons which can be cited in corroboration, this conclusion is to be held as correct. The first is certainly that prescriptions of property proceed from the law of conscience so that personal legal action is prescribed by the passage of 30 years. It follows that this action was prescribed and that legal action cannot be brought against the tutor or administrator because so much time has passed, especially as prescriptions were created by both canon and civil law in order to avoid subsequent litigation and costs. The second reason: the account is considered rendered when it can be assisted or proven by a verisimilar and favorable explanation. Then it is proven, following what is said. The third: when something cannot be determined by witnesses or writings, it can be determined by natural reason, which reason directly disposes and orders all things and causes the conscience remorse when something is done against reason. This natural reason is more than the surface of the written words inasmuch as it is licit to argue on the basis of natural reason without alleging any law whatsoever. The law is based on reason and thus natural reason can be alleged in judicial decisions, so that a law exists which determines that a period of 30 years prescribes the account which the tutor or administrator is required to give. The gloss[3] and the doctors omitted this law, but the above arguments and natural reason support it. The lord of the administered goods and afterwards his children and heirs did not request the goods for such a long time that they are considered paid and for this reason the laws are said to succor the watchful and not those who sleep.}

This is true except where the master or partner did not request the account from the administrator or copartner; then it will suffice that the administrator or partner should render account at the time it is requested, the year having passed.

But if it was agreed between the master and the administrator that he render account at a certain time, it will suffice that the administrator render account at the agreed time. He cannot be compelled to render it before, even though the year of which we spoke above or even longer may have passed.

Except in the case where the keeper of the goods should administer them badly and not as he ought; or make himself suspicious, dissipating his own goods, gambling with them, or using them for dishonest purposes. In badly using his own goods, it is presumed that he will use another's in an even worse manner. In this case, he will render account before the agreed time arrives and in other similar cases, such as when the administrator wants to absent himself for a long time far from his province.

Furthermore, where the lord requests the account from his administrator or the partner from his copartner because they know that the administrator or copartner has the account book in other parts where they had just cause to carry it and that in such a short time as a year they would not be able to bring it back as would happen with many merchants who do business in Flanders of this land[4] and in other areas; in this case they would not be culpable although a year may have passed since they had rendered account.

Another case in which the administrator is not obliged to render an account to his master is when thirty years have passed after the termination of his administration. Except if he were the administrator of a church or monastery for which he is obligated up to 40 years to render account.

Likewise, once the administrator has given account to his master, solemnly and as he ought, and the account appears as I said in the fourth part of this tract, he will not be obliged to render account again. I said solemnly and as he ought because if he rendered account to someone to whom he did not have to render it or he lacked any of the requirements for rendering the account, he does not in fact exhibit it. It is as if he did not render it; but if he rendered account before the proper person and as he ought, the administrator will not be obligated to render it again. Except where the account having been made, one of the parties were to say that they see an error in it; then it would have to be examined again in the manner which is revealed in the tenth part of this treatise.

Some want to say as well that the administrator need not render account when the lord releases him from giving it. Others say that the guardian must render account to his ward even though the testator in his testament might have ordered that he not render it. Others say that this remission does not free the administrator from paying what he owes; nor does it free him if he committed some fraud or deceit against his master in the administration that he had of his goods, hiding or stealing some part of them, although it may work provided that they do not take a strict or very narrow accounting. This third opinion is more accepted; and if it is true many administrators fool themselves thinking that when masters order their heirs in their testaments or in another manner not to take account of the administration that the administrators had that they are free from rendering it; and in my opinion they are not free, particularly where a strict accounting is not taken. Except where the lord clearly considers the administrator as free and the account as verified, then the administrator should not render account of the administration he held in any manner. In such a case the administrator will be as free as if he had already rendered account, in the same way that the master releases him and considers him as quit of the account when the administrator pays any outstanding balance. {Furthermore, there is the question whether the testator can release the heir or executor from making an inventory of the goods that he bequeathed. Certain doctors say yes, except where it is necessary to the public good that the inventory be made; then such a release is invalid.}

Part Six

As for the sixth part in which we reveal where or in what place the account must be rendered. Briefly we can say that the account must be rendered where the administration was held.

If the administrator is not in the place that he held the administration but in another jurisdiction or place, he has to be sent to the place where he held the administration so that there he may render account of the goods that he administered. And if you would like to know why he has to be sent back, I say for two reasons. The first, by absenting himself from the place where he held the administration, he committed a delict because he must remain until the account is rendered. And on account of the delict, the judge of first instance is the one where it was committed. And as before this judge the release must be made, so before him the administrator may render account of the goods that he administered or the charge he held.

Another reason makes clearer and more evident why the administrator must render account in the place where he administered the goods: it is because the law presumes that where contracted, the truth is better able to be known.

If the lord wants to come before the judge with the administrator in the place where he has absented himself, the administrator has to request the release. The reason for this is because the release is not made principally in favor of the master but so that the truth about the two parties may be better investigated.

An exception is where both consent, they can render account before another judge, and then to them falls any advantage or harm of the arrangement.

Part Seven

As for the seventh part in which we relate: what things the account book must contain so that it is considered well ordered. I say that it has to have written first all that the administrator received from his master. Secondly, all that he gave to his master and to others at his command; and what he spent on his person and on behalf of his master's property, his business dealings and lawsuits.

And the administrator's account book that does not contain payments and receipts is not well ordered and creates suspicion against the administrator so that he is obliged to pay his master the interest that might be proven. If the administrator were not to write down all that he receives from the lord's debtors, the administrator must pay double. And this payment and receipt of which we spoke above, taken together, is called *libro de cuentas.*

And although this may be true, it is not to be understood that payments and receipts must of necessity be written and set down in one book or volume; it is sufficient that the receipts be set down in one volume and the payments or expenditures in another; and each book is called account book whether it contains payments or receipts. In every respect it is better that receipts and expenditures are set down in one volume so that suspicion does not arise against the administrator, that he removed or added some entry, increasing expenditures or committing other frauds while he was away.

And if the administrator is treasurer, *contador* or receiver of the royal rents and taxes, he has to put at the end of the account book the name of the reigning prince and the day on which he receives the taxes, rents and other goods of his master and the day, month and year in which he gave, spent or paid them.

Likewise, it is required that the administrators put in the entries the reason that they gave or spent the *maravedis* or things that they have set down in the account book so that the *contadores* can know if the cause of the expenditure was just or sufficient.

Similarly, it is necessary that the administrator write in the account book extensively and in detail what he spent, and on what he spent it and to whom he gave and paid it.

{What we say regarding these other administrators we can say about any testator who by his testament or in some other way should leave his goods or crops or a certain quantity of them to be sold in order to ransom captives, enable orphans to marry or to be distributed to the poor; that the bishop to whom it pertains to accomplish these pious works or the person whom the testator committed must set down in a register or inventory all those goods that come into their possession and the day, month and year they received them. The year of receipt having past, he who received the goods must render an account of them before the secular judge of whatever jurisdiction was named by the testator, including how many captives were ransomed, how many women married, how many poor people given alms and the sum given to each. This has to be rendered publicly and in this work no money profit is required.}

And if the administrator's book should not have written the day, month and year in which he received the master's goods; and the day on which he gave, spent or distributed them and the reason for the expenditure, the account would be confused and could not be counted rightly. And such an account would cause suspicion against the administrator. And therefore he would be culpable and with some other indication he might incur a penalty. And the *contadores* could not pass the entry which did not have the things cited above; because the account, being as is said confused and obscure, the *contadores* could not understand nor know if some fraud or trick had occurred in it. And not being able to know the truth well they could not justly pass what had been set down.

From which it follows that the *contadores* don't have to give any credence to the administrator's book except when in addition to the payment and receipts each entry contains the day, month and year in which he says the expenditure was made and the cause of the expenditure.

This is true where the lord denies what is contained in some entry; but if he should recognize it or confess to it, it has to be approved, because the lord's admission removes all suspicion.

Similarly, it is true that the entry in which the day, month and year and the reason do not appear, does not have to be received as part of the account when the entry is one in which the administrator says what he gave, spent, or paid or says some other thing in his own favor. But if he says he received, even though he has not put down on what day, such an entry has to be accepted against the administrator. And thus we say that in receipts the day is not required but for payments, yes. We say the same about the cause, that although with expenditures the reason has to be expressed, it is not neccesary with receipts.

And when some cause of expenditure is named, the *contadores* have to watch that it is just and sufficient, because only a very strict and urgent reason should move the *contador* to pass the expenditure.

And I advise *contadores* not to pass the costs or expenditures that the administrators say they have incurred except where the reason for the expenditure is clearly evident, saying what they spent and on what and why they spent it. And if it seems to the *contadores* the reason for the expenditure is not sufficient, they will not pass the expenditure. An example is a house the administrator has built. The administrator says that he knocked it down and built it again. The *contadores* have to know why he knocked it down, the house having already been built; and if he says that he knocked it down because it was about to fall down, this is a just reason; and should the administrator prove it, it will be sufficient in order for them to pass what appears a just and proper expenditure. And if it is not proven that it was a necessity to knock the house down, then they will not pass the expenditure, because the reason for it was not just but confused and wrong.

And thus the collectors of the royal taxes are obliged to send in writing to the court how much they collected and on what they spent it and in what manner and the reason and the amount they spent. They have to identify by his proper name whom they paid.

And thus with the account named, the administrators and collectors of the royal taxes have to receive copies of what they have been ordered to collect, noting in their turn that "I collected from Pedro so many *maravedis* and from Juan so many" and thus when they collect they have to set down in writing that they collected from Pedro so much and from Juan so much. And thus it is done in this realm in the collection of the *moneda forera*[1] and other taxes and in the places which compounded the *alcabalas* and *tercias*[2] of their highnesses. When the districts allot the taxes among them, they give to each receiver or collector one written copy of what they are ordered to collect from each householder and thus the collector or receiver sets down in writing what he has collected from each one.

And if the account is not rendered or verified in this manner, those who receive it could not recognize nor understand if the receiver, collector, tutor, guardian or any other administrator had committed some fraud in it. I have seen and found with others delegated by commission of those very lofty and most Christian princes Don Fernando and Dona Isabel, King and Queen, our lords of glorious memory[3], to examine a receiver's account that in the expenditures and costs that the receiver said he had made, he had counted and set down in the account book one item three times and the one entry was well separated from the other and said thus: On the first of May in the year 1500 I gave to Goncalo Hernandez ten thousand *maravedis* on the order of the lord justices and *regidores* because he was at the court of their highnesses. And in another entry he said, on the first of May in the year 1500 I gave to Goncalo Hernandez five thousand *maravedis* on the order of the lord justices and *regidores* because he was at the court of their highnesses and in another entry he said in the same way that he had given to him five thousand *maravedis* and for the same reason.

So that if they pass these three entries, the receiver will unjustly make off with ten thousand *maravedis*. But having seen the date on which he was paid and the reason that he was at the court of their highnesses, it was ascertained that there was only one journey and they did not release more than ten thousand *maravedis*.

Also we find in the account book of certain collectors of the *alcabalas*, in the time when these kingdoms compounded them, which was in the year 1499, that they collected and gathered a much greater quantity than what was originally ordered they should collect; which showed up when the copy that they were given, on the basis of which they were to collect, was viewed together with their book of receipts, that is, the bills and acquittances we had brought to the debtors who paid the *alcabala*.

And for this reason I say that the persons deputed to take account from others ought to be cautious and well-informed in examining them and be strongly warned, because many administrators render an entry and afterwards they render it many more times in detail and they double and redouble the expenditures that they actually made only once. And if they spent two *maravedis*, they say three and such as these ought to be doubly punished.

And on account of these it is said that many officials and administrators are wolves, robbers and dogs of court who in diverse ways and with big tricks and deceits behead the sheep so quickly they don't even feel it and drink their blood.

And I even say, on account of what I saw, that they don't content themselves with the blood, but also they eat the meat right to the bone and they would eat even that except that it might be too hard; so they leave it thinking that they will put new meat on top and eat again. And if you think about it, everywhere you can find many rich administrators who before had no goods and I have seen them. Also it is said that such administrators and receivers know the poor lords, short of funds and in debt, and commit much more wrongdoing than others. It is because money blinds administrators, making them covet as their own the money of others.

Part Eight

As for the eighth part in which we relate what things lend credence to the administrator's book and what do not. Because this part is one of the principal parts of this tract, I divide it into three sections.

The first is, or we ask, if the account book constitutes evidence in favor of the person who wrote it.

Or if it is evidence against the person who wrote it.

Or against another person.

As for the first: if it is evidence in favor of the person who wrote it. Some say that in the things that depend on the consent of the one who wrote it, it is good evidence. As it would be in a writing if one were to say: I leave and bequest my goods to the poor and the church.

There are three opinions if it is a matter that does not depend on the consent of the one who wrote it, except where the office obligates him to what he writes. One of these opinions proves nothing. If it was a writing of some deceased person who was a good man, then with other indications or presumptions they say that it proves entirely in favor of the administrator.

There is another opinion: that the writings of merchants although written in their favor are supporting evidence and that with the merchant's oath they make confirming evidence. And this opinion does not satisfy other scholars nor anyone else. Before they condemn it by means of a reason that seems good to me, they say thus: that a writing cannot make more or prove more than one can with his own voice. Therefore it is certain that the speech of a man under oath who expresses something in his own favor does not constitute supporting evidence. No one ought to be believed or can be a witness in his own favor even though he may be a man of great dignity or of much authority. It is certain then that if we were to hold the second opinion, it would be an ugly and absurd thing, that all proof should depend on one lone man believing in the book that he himself wrote and in his oath, it being well known that according to divine and human law at least two witnesses are necessary in order to make complete proof in favor of others. More proof is required in favor of he who testifies because there is more suspicion; and where there is more suspicion better proof is required. And were credence to be given to a person on account of his book and oath, we would oppose it with two witness and it would still make better evidence in his case than in that of another, which is not just.

There is a third opinion, that the administrator's writing or of any person considered along with other signs is proof in favor of the one who wrote it; on the other hand, they say, it may not be. And they give an example, saying: It is certain that the confession one makes in the absence of the party it concerns does not harm the one confessing even though the notary of the cause may set the confession down in writing in the other writs of the process. And if this is true, they say that it ought to be worth less when someone in his chamber in the absence of the other party were to write in his book whatever he wants. Others respond to this reasoning, saying it does not pertain to our case because the confession we cited was simple even though the notary set it down in writing. But in our case there is a writing that always speaks, which when it comes into your possession can speak with you, likewise as we say about the letter that I send to you, that it is proof.

Some limit this, saying that it has no place in the case where someone made another write the account book, that it would not prove against him if it is reckoned in the absence of the other party; likewise as we said about the confession that is made in court in the absence of the other party and is put down in writing. And they say that the letter that I send to another who is absent is one thing; confessing anything in it is seen as confessing it in the presence of the one to whom I send the letter since I send the letter so that he may see it. And the book that is inscribed in the absence of the other party is quite another thing; he who writes it did not have the intention of confessing what he writes in the presence of the other party and on account of this any such admission that is made in the account book would not harm the one who wrote it.

Finally, returning to the doctors' opinions on those two articles that we related above, whether the account book proves in favor of the one who wrote it or against the one who wrote it; they say and conclude that if he who wrote it is a man of good reputation, it makes supporting proof and that with other indications it proves entirely in favor of the one who wrote it.

But that against him who wrote the book, the book proves entirely without other sign or any other proof.

While a merchant or administrator or some other person might write in his book that a person deposited with him 100 thousand *maravedis* and in another entry of the same book write that of those 100 thousand *maravedis* he had restored and paid 50 thousand *maravedis*, the person who says that he made the deposit will be able to receive what the merchant says he deposited before him and not receive what he says he paid to the merchant. And thus we say that the book proves against the one who wrote it and not in his favor.

{Note that the private or simple writing proves entirely against the one who wrote it (acknowledged as the one who wrote it) while it can be carried out if it contains a certain sum, without proceeding to sentence.[1] Some people write, saying in their letter, "Master Fulano, you know well that you owe me so many *maravedis*." I say that if the person who receives the letter, which is in his book or otherwise in his possession, does not show or prove the contrary, he will be compelled to pay what is contained in the letter.

It is true that credence has to be given to a lesser extent than may seem likely to the account book of a tutor, guardian or administrator even though he is a man of good repute; but having been examined by a judge, it ought to be believed and not otherwise.

Lastly, note that the tutor, guardian, administrator or executor of a testament is obligated for anything that he may have done or failed to do on account of fraud or gross negligence.

From here we say also that a person can testify against himself but not in his own favor. And if in the administrator's book it is said: I received 100 thousand *maravedis* more or less, such an admission would harm the administrator's interest in those 100 thousand *maravedis*; although some want to say that this admission is uncertain and that the uncertain admission can do no harm.

The third article, whether the account book is proof against a third party. Some doctors say that if the account book was dated by public authority as *contadores* do, to whom is given entire credence because they write down in the account books by royal authority, such a book is proof.

Not only when it affirms that one paid but also it is authentic testimony if it should say that someone did not pay.

And if the account book is not kept on account of some public office, then it is not proof.

Except where by statute or custom it is given complete credence, then such a book is proof.

And here we say today that if they are men of good repute, the books of the royal *contadores*, because they are approved by royal authority, and likewise the account books of the money changers and other merchants who swear on their art and office, because they succeed those who had public office, make supporting evidence even though they hold no public office.

The laws that say that an authentic writing is supporting evidence are understood to mean that the person who made it was honorable and of good reputation.

And it is to be noted that when the merchant or money changer is licensed, his book makes complete proof. But if the merchant takes on his own volition the office of merchant or money changer as the merchants, storekeepers and others who sell publicly do today in this kingdom, his book does not make complete proof in his favor nor against others nor even supporting proof. Because such a merchant or storekeeper is a private person and not a public person.

And likewise I have frequently seen in lawsuits cloth merchants and shopkeepers who say they have sold to others on credit and request from them sums of *maravedis*. And they present their books in proof of what they said and neither complete nor even a moderate amount of belief was given their book. With a witness and the merchant's oath they find in his favor in the case of a small or moderate sum but not in any other way.

But where one wrote in his book on the order of another who owes to him so many *maravedis* it will make proof against the person who ordered him to write, it alone proving the order that he set down in writing what was owed or how much given. And likewise I have seen some people who took merchandise and said to the merchant that he should set down in his book that he owed the merchant so many *maravedis* for cloth that he sold to him. And this is done many times between laborers, students and even squires who have money infrequently and merchants from whom they take something on credit. And on this the doctors who speak on this subject conclude. If with their pronouncements we now pass from the said three articles, we would have as many doubts now after seeing them as before.

Subject to emendation and correction of those who are most concerned to know the truth, I make of this next part another major distinction.

Let us ask what things lend credence to an account book and what things do not.

Let us ask how something is proven which is not proven by the account book.

As for the first, credence will be given to the account book. Regarding the things that the administrator received from his master complete credence is given to the account book against the interests of the administrator, according to what is said above. But if the administrator says through his account book that he collected from so-and-so so many *maravedis*, it is doubtful if credence will be given to such a book because anyone is free to say that he received and collected so much. I say that if such an administrator is from the *fisco* [public treasury] his book is proof of payment even though the admission of the administrator may be less solemn. But if he who made this admission was the proxy of some private person and he had power to collect and to give acquittances even though he may say that he collected, it should not prove that he paid over the collections to his master; the proxy's admission does not prejudice the lord's interests. And since the proxy in the written instrument may have the power to admit what he receives and were he to confess having received, the admission would not harm the lord. No matter how cautious he may be, he who pays another's proxy should make the payment before a notary or witnesses and have the notary set it down in the acquittance that he paid in his presence and that of the witnesses and the same if anyone should pay the guardian or caretaker of another person.

And let us speak about the necessity of proving those things that the administrator says he gave or spent. Let us say that if the payment, expense or cost was of a great enough quantity that a public writing can be made of it, I say that the expenditure has to be proven completely with witnesses or writings and this is the reason: that administrators know or ought to know that they must render account. They ought to safeguard themselves for what they might spend or pay by paying it in the presence of someone who can prove it or they should take a writing of what they paid or gave and by whose order it was done.

So, in the expenditure of a great sum credence will not be given to the administrator's book alone nor with his oath even though he may be or may have been a man of good repute and of much credit and honor.

In the second case when the expenditure or cost is small in amount or is made up of many smaller payments as in the expenditures that tutors make for their wards so that they can eat and clothe themselves; or the steward or dispenser makes in providing for his master so that he and his family can eat; or in the expenditures that they make for the building of forts and houses and for the work of field, vineyard and livestock and other similar tasks; of such expenditures a public writing cannot be made nor can the amount that was spent be proven by witnesses. I say that if such costs are verisimilar or appear evident, they are proven by the account book together with the administrator's oath if he is still alive.

The same would hold when the costs can be proven by reason as we spoke of above. If the guardian or caretaker gives to his ward so that he can eat and dress, naturally two or more persons can see and judge that that ward could not continue living without food and clothing and they can measure intuitively what the guardian could spend each year on the ward. And thus they could ascertain if what the guardian says that he spent in detail on his ward is verisimilar or naturally increasing; and then even though the individual expenditures may add up to a great sum, credence will be given to the administrator's book along with his oath.

And thus we say that costs can be proven by sight and by an intuitive knowledge. So that if the guardian or administrator might say that he spent 1000 ducats on building a house, those who might see the house and know how much in those parts the lumber, lime, stone, nails, the wages of masons and carpenters and other things in the house cost can know if the expenditure on the house that the administrator says he has made is true or not. And this proof and investigation, having been made in full understanding of the facts, is sufficient without witnesses or writings; and in this the administrator's book will be believed.

Likewise costs can be proven by other surmises which occur to the judge before whom the question is debated; of what these surmises consist of in fact no fixed rule can be given.

And for this reason I say that the doctors' conclusion and opinion is not good in as far as they said that if the administrator had been a good man, they have to give credence to his book; because as it turns out we don't have to give consideration to whether he may be a good man or not, only to the quantity of the expenditure, whether it is big or small. If the expenditure, even though it may be large, has been set down in detail, even though it is true that there is some doubt about the verisimilitude of the expenditure, more credence is given to the book of the administrator who was or is a good man than to the book of one who was not such a man.

Also, an expenditure is proven by the writing in which the judge or lord ordered the administrator to make a payment, or a cost by the acquittance of someone who was ordered to give or pay; which proof is surer and more certain than another. In order to be more certain, I advise tutors, guardians, and other administrators that if someone other than their lord should demand from them money or some other thing, they should not give or pay it without an order or letter from their master or a judge; because through a defect in proof or for having paid what the lord did not owe or had cause for not paying, the *contadores* will not approve it as part of the account. I say that before they consent to pay, for justice's sake they should request that they be ordered to pay by judicial sentence so that they have proof, so that there may be no doubt if they paid justly or if they can prove it.

So that it is good to take a bill, warrant or writ from the master describing how he ordered payment and an acquittance of how he paid because written evidence is proof because it proves what he says.

And if for example the lord should write to the administrator in the following manner, "Here is Fulano; believe what he tells you." If some lad said to the administrator that the lord ordered the administrator to give to him so many thousand *maravedis*, this letter would be enough for the administrator to be free to give him the money

It is true that when the debt is clear the administrator can pay it. But because there can be some debate between the lord and the administrator whether the debt was clear, the administrator ought to avoid becoming embroiled in the quarrel in the first place, because the administrator should recognize that regarding a known debt there can be cause for which the administrator should pay what he paid from his own goods. I give an example: In these kingdoms, in all the cities or towns, or in the greater part of them, the salaries of governors, *assistentes*, *corregidores*, *veynti quatros*, *regidores*, *jurados* and other municipal officials are known. And the steward or receiver could pay the *corregidor* his salary because it is well known what is owed to him and thus they pay it without any warrant whatsoever; but if for example the *assistente*, *corregidor* or *regidor* may have been absent from his office for longer than the permitted time, they would have to prorate his salary. But if he were to have paid for anything it will not excuse the receiver from having to pay it from his own goods and they will not take it into account because he paid what he ought not to.

And many want to say that officials cannot pay one *maravedi* on their own initiative except where there is a real obligation against their lord.

And because some could say that the expenditure is either of a great or small quantity so that the administrator's book may have the opportunity of being believed, I say that this is left to the discretion of he who has to judge the case, having seen the quality of the parties and of the goods which were given in administration and of the costs and the thing on which they were expended and having had some consideration for the time at which the expenditure was made.

And if for example the lord and the administrator should differ over some small amount that the administrator said that he gave to his master; and the master denies it, I say that the lord's oath on whether he received some sum and not that of the administrator has to be relied on. Except were it the case that the lord was known as a man of bad character and dealings and the administrator was a man of good repute, then the *contadores* would accept the oath of the administrator and not that of the master.

Part Nine

As for the ninth part in which we relate: what administrators can do by reason of their office and what they cannot.

I say that by order of the master or of a judge they can pay what is contained in the master's or judge's warrant.

Likewise they can pay themselves their salary and all the rest that is owed to them by reason of the goods that they administered. Just as administrators can pay to others what is rightly owed to them, they can pay themselves.

Also they can sell or transfer all those things that perish over time, especially when they are so old that soon they are ruined and lost; thus as it would be with wheat, oil, wine, meat, fruit and vegetables and other things that are quickly ruined and lost. And if for example they were not sold in time and they were lost, the administrator must pay for them from his own goods even though the master may not have given him power to sell them.

{And not only will the tutor, guardian or administrator be able to sell the aforementioned fruits; they can also sell them without the authority or decree of a judge. The reason they have to sell is as said above, so that the fruits might not perish or be lost. Note they are not obliged to reserve or keep the fruits so that they can be sold when they are most dear or when they are worth the most nor are they obligated to carry them to other parts outside of the area where the fruits are located; but they have to sell them where the fruits are located and for an average price. Also, the tutor or guardian can spend all that may be necessary on the marriage of his ward.

Know, too, that the ward's tutor or guardian can spend all that is necessary on the nuptials of the ward's sister or on his poor relatives if his financial condition permits.

Also, it often happens, and I have seen it, that the tutor, guardian or administrator has gone over to live in the house of his ward or of the master whose goods he administers; it is doubtful if at the time the account is rendered the judge or *contadores* would order that he be charged a yearly rent for the house.

Others would say yes, since he lived in the house, especially if he had his own house in which he might have lived. The truth is that if in any way it is more convenient to the ward, wards or to the master of the goods of which he had the administration for the tutor or administrator to live in the master's house, the tutor or administrator will not be obligated to pay anything to live there. For example, in a case where the father or mother of minors had a good house and left their sons or daughters in it and the tutor's house was not as good; or because it was improper to take the minors from their father's house: or because the father was a prominent man and it was more just for the administrator to go and live where the master lived than the contrary. In this the judge's discretion can better consider the issue because in law there is no certain rule.

I have found myself in the confidence of a grandee of the realm who is a minor of 25 years and has a *cavallero*[1] as a guardian. At Easter the guardian made a donation or donations of 100 thousand *maravedis* as *de juro perpetuo*[2] on his master's behalf. It was disputed among his attorneys whether the 100 thousand *maravedis* had to be accounted for. My opinion was that upon this issue we had to make a distinction, whether the right was given for a stupid reason, whether it was given to a man or woman, or for a just cause that could move the lord to make the contribution himself. In the first case the guardian could not make the donation unless it were a much smaller sum; in the second case I said that the guardian could make use of the said liberality and largesse, a just, honest and reasonable cause preceding it and consideration having been had for the dignity and grandeur of the master and of his rents. They also concluded in this way.

Also, based on the aforementioned case it can be said that the tutor, guardian and administrator of any other person of lesser condition than the grandee can make a small donation from the goods of his ward or master provided that a just cause as above exists; especially if what was given was to a poor person or for the service of God. Any son in the power of his father who has administration of a small sum and any prelate who feels it justly spent could do the same. Where the tutor or administrator being poor or in need cannot administer the goods without maintaining himself from them, he can do so.

Likewise if he has a dispute with another regarding something touching his master's affairs and the justice of the matter is doubtful, the administrator will place this dispute in the hands of other individuals for determination and in this way the administrator will be able to reconcile himself with the other party.

Which is true except where the administrator should fake having such a dispute regarding his master's affairs; then the transaction the administrator might make would not be valid.

It is said that the administrator who can compromise and amicably agree when there is occasion, that administrator is such that he has free administration as the father has in the goods of his child or as another who has authority with free administration and with the discretion of the judge.

Also he can abandon the suit upon which they plead on oath of the one with whom he litigates or with whom he has the dispute where he does not have the evidence of witnesses or of writings with which to help himself and the suit is doubtful.

Also when the administrator sells some of the master's things which the law permits, clearly he can sell them at auction.

Where he is administrator of a church or monastery, he cannot buy them in any manner.

Also he can renew the instrument or contract of the lord which is broken.

He can repair and rebuild some residence or fortress or mill which is broken and ruined or about to fall provided that the judge should see it or has it seen and declares that it is necessary to repair the building.

Also he can transfer his own goods.

Also he can pawn the lord's goods on his order.

Likewise he can remit or pardon the master's debt which is disputed because such a remission is not a donation. But I advise tutors and guardians that they should not remit or pardon or let loose on that account any debt that may be owed to the lord since the remission, even though it may not be a donation, is a manner or type of transfer. Which the guardian or administrator cannot do without a just or necessary cause and with the decree or authority of the judge.

Also he can give to his ward's instructor such a sum that should satisfy the instructor for the work he did in teaching the ward.

And generally he can do all that appears to be to the utility and advantage of his master. So that if he goes to other parts on the ward's or master's business, he can take from those goods that he administers what is neceesary for his maintenance. Except where by law the administrator is set a certain salary because then he could not collect more than that, as it is with the salaries of tutors.

But if the administrator gave or paid some sum which the lord did not owe, it will not be accepted as part of the account.

Also if the guardian or administrator commits usury with the money of Christ, the administrator or guardian must restore or pay from his own goods what he unjustly gained.

Also if he were not to pay on time what the lord owes and he incurs costs because of this, the administrator will be held and obliged to pay them from his own goods. And not from the lord's goods.

Also if he was negligent in collecting the debts that are owed to his master and the debtors fled, the administrator shall pay them from his own goods. But if the administrator were to prove that he could not demand repayment of the debts because of a just impediment that he had, and the debtors fled at this time, the administrator will not be obliged to pay the debts because he was not to blame. In order for the administrator to be obligated, the master has to prove that it was the administrator's fault that the debtor fled, because the law presumes that the administrator was not to blame. But if the lord were to prove that the time for the debtor to pay had come, and the administrator let pass so much time that there was opportunity for the debtor to lose his goods or flee with them, this proof would be sufficient to demonstrate that the administrator was to blame in not collecting the debt in time; and on account of his culpability he would have to pay it.

Also, if the administrator contracted with some person who had not paid some sum, and the debtor flees and the debt cannot be collected, the administrator must pay the lord from his own goods.

And even in the case where the administrator contracted with someone many times before and he had the money to pay and he fled with the lord's debts, the administrator will be obligated to pay them because he was to blame for having contracted with this person in the first place.

Except where the guardian or administrator asked the mother or relatives of the ward or master whether he should trust such merchandise to Fulano or whether he should contract with him and they said yes, in such a case even if the debtor fled with the debt, the administrator will not be obligated to pay it.

Also he cannot let go nor remit the debt which is undisputed and clearly owed to the master even though the debt is irksome and the administrator is a lawful man. It is understood that he cannot expressly remit it, the administrator saying I have let you go from such a debt that you owe the lord whose administrator I am. But quietly he can leave off from seeking repayment of the debt so that he in effect remits it. And this could be done in this way: the lord could leave off seeking repayment of the debt for a period of time or space of ten, twenty or thirty years; according to the condition or quality of the debt it is lost and prescribed by this space of time. And this period having passed, the master could not seek repayment of the debt on account of it having been prescribed. But in this case it is held as certain that the lord, even though he cannot seek the debt from the debtor, could collect it from the administrator for having been negligent in collecting it and allowing it to be lost by the passage of time.

Also if the administrator sues recklessly or against the interests of justice he ought to pay the costs and not the lord; and the sentence has to be carried out on the goods of the administrator.

Also he cannot compromise so that the judges might sentence amicably.

Also he cannot pawn one of the master' possessions unless it may be to the utility and advantage of the lord.

Also he cannot trifle or amuse himself with something that belongs to his master.

Also he cannot dissipate or badly bargain with or destroy the lord's goods.

Also if he extorts more from the lord's debtors than what they owe, he ought to be doubly punished.

Also if he did not write in his book what he received or collected he must pay it twice.

Also the official or administrator cannot remit the privileges that are owed to his master.

Also if he is negligent in collecting what is owed to his lord he does not have to be paid any salary.

Also the official cannot request nor collect the sums that are owed to the lord from *alcabalas* and other things without first showing his book to the debtors.

Some might doubt what has been said. The tutor wanted to sell or transfer some of the ward's goods and sold them with the authority of the judge. In the sale the legal requirements were not observed. The buyer fled with the purchases. In case the lord wants to have recourse, could he have it against the tutor or against the judge? I say that the tutor has to pay, that he has to have recourse first against the tutor. In order not to pay, the tutor can collect from the judge because he gave him license to sell the ward's goods without a just cause.

You can take as a general rule that all administrators are obligated to their lord for collecting the debts from the debtors whatever misfortune or great blame they incur.

And some times officials are obligated for what they did to the detriment of the lord and for what they left off from doing on account of negligence. And you can give an example where another more diligent administrator could have been found to take the administration.

Part Ten

As for the tenth part in which we discuss whether an account has to be reexamined, recounted and withdrawn if it is in error.

I say that just as errors which are sometimes made in confessions do not harm the informer or confessant and can be revoked, thus an error found in the account does not cause any damage, but the account has to be examined again if any of the parties request it.

{In some places where there is not a great abundance of livestock, the cattlemen, who are called *señores de ganado*, customarily join their livestock together and hold it in a partnership in order to avoid the cost and expense of the shepherds or people who guard the herd. And thus it is that having to give to the shepherd three or four thousand *maravedis* to watch 200 or 300 head of livestock, they can get a shepherd's helper, a young boy, to watch 600 or 800 and pass on the cost to the partnership. One of the them brought to the partnership 500 head and the other 300; the partnership having ended, they distributed to each 300 and all the other things that they had in the herd; they didn't distribute more because the other 200 head were dead as it appears according to the account or book of the shepherd or foreman. Time having passed, the one who put in the 500 head or his heirs request that the one who put in 300 head or his heirs give or pay for the 200 head that are lacking in order to complete the 500 head that he placed in partnership, along with the fruits or products that would have resulted after the division was made. Those of whom the request is made answer that the division or distribution was made and that it is unnecessary to request it again nor is what is requested from them necessary. The heirs of the one who put in the 500 head reply that the distribution was in error because in truth he had to have the other 200 head in order not to oppose the division that was made.

The other party replies that there was no error because those 200 head were compensated for and were given in compensation for the difference in quality. It was better that they held the 30 [*sic*] head that their father gave which were two-year olds or yearlings and of very fine wool; the 500 head that the other put in were fenced in or yoked and of inferior wool. For this reason he was seen to have put in 500 in order to equal the quality of the 300. Thus, in the division equality was observed. On the other hand it is said that this equality is considered or is held to have been considered in respect of the number of the livestock and not of the quality or value of it; if the partner sees that his copartner does not put in beasts as good as his own he has to protest so that equality is preserved. Otherwise he was seen to consent tacitly to the division, distribution and partnership that they contracted. But this observation concerning the protest does not apply since the protest was not made; were it clearly made, consent will be shown to be excluded. But unless the protest was made, it does not always follow that he consented, so that the silence is prejudicial to him. Silence in prejudicial acts does not produce consent when *reverencia*[1] is owed by the protester because in such a case he is presumed to contradict and not to consent. There is this exception because such a situation could occur between the vassals of some lord. I have seen that the *pecheros* [commoners] subject to the favorites or principals of some lord don't dare to protest against them. Taking from them or asking of them part of their property even down to the small change, the *pecheros* don't dare but to give it to them. If the one who put in the old, thin, rough and yellowish stock was the lord's favorite or principal as I have said and the one who put in the 300 good head was from below, it follows that the silence is not prejudicial to him. Thus, the doubt remains if there is some qualification between the partners, whether the issue has to be considered solely in respect of the quality and value of the livestock. Some could say that consideration has to be had only for the numbers and not for the quality or value of the stock.

Because the partnership is understood to be held in equal parts; if the one who put in 300 head has to put in 500 like his copartner and then does not do so, each must take out the number of animals that he put in. But the contrary opinion seems more reasonable and conforms to good conscience, and it is that this partnership is considered not only in respect of the number of livestock but also in terms of quality and value. I base this opinion on the following foundation:

The first, that the partnership has to have in itself great goodness. Certainly, such goodness would not be presumed if in the partnership consideration were given only to the number and not to the quality of the thing and on this basic assumption, the good intention, conscience and office of the judge and his discretion depend.

The second, that the estimation of a thing is the same as the thing itself so that to put in 100 ewes is as much as putting in 200 if the 100 are worth as much as the 200. Whence it is said that the one who is obligated to hand over wheat can give his estimation of its value. And for this reason some doctors say that the estimation succeeds in place of the thing and the estimation is held as the thing itself. Also the doctors say that the estimation of the property does not have to be made or the property does not have to be appraised in respect of the number or bushels of crop that can be sown but more according to the goodness or value of the property. Thus in our case this equality ought not to be considered solely in respect of the number but also of the livestock's worth. Accordingly, between the partners strict equality is preserved and the division having been made, it cannot be said that there is error in it. It is necessary that the value of the stock or of the other products is legitimately proven so that the division is considered entirely just. If it were not proved entirely, then the judge on account of his office would estimate. I would judge in the present case that the division was justly made and that the estimation or appraisal was made by both partners, as was said, since between them they made the division right down to the dogs, pots and everything else they had in the herd. Thus, it is presumed that the division was made.

Also it is said that in deeds the intention is understood.

Also in this case it has to be considered whether the one who put in 300 head had charge of inspecting the livestock and the shepherds, finding them food and examining the accounts and whether he put in this the work of his person and of those of his household in cooking the bread, all of which it is just to consider. The other partner was quiet, leaving to others the conduct of his transactions and suits; a long period had passed after the distribution was made, and this partner made no claim. All of which the judge has to consider in order to determine whether the distribution was well made or whether there was an error in it.}

And here note that if some merchants examined, summed and verified their accounts often, anyone who was shorted by them could say the accounts contained an error and could ask that they be examined again, reviewed and looked over to see if there is an error.

Which is true since there exists a stipulation regarding what is counted, summed and verified. Which stipulation is caused in the following manner. The creditor says to the debtor, promise to pay me on such and such a day so many *maravedis* that you owe on this account; and the debtor might say that he promises it. Since the debtor made the promise he can request that the accounts be looked at again to see if there is an error in them.

Except where, the account having been examined, the parties asked the judge to pass sentence and order the debtor to pay the outstanding balance after so many days. But if there was a settlement between them, in such a case the accounts would not be done again even though one of the parties might say that the accounts contained an error. Such a compromise might be caused in the following manner: the lord and the administrator disputed something and they agreed to apportion and divide it in a certain manner. If afterwards one of them should say that the account was in error, it will not be reexamined because the two had already agreed.

And when the account is reexamined because of an error, it has to be reviewed by two people; each of the parties has to name one of them. And if either of the parties should not want to name an individual, the judge on the petition of the other party will compel him to name someone. And if on the order of the judge, the party still does not want to name someone, the judge can make the appointment, and protect what the two appointees might find out. And if for example the parties name two people to review the accounts and they do not agree on the results of the review, the judge can set an intermediary and transfer the investigation that the two made.

And the persons appointed to review the accounts have to swear that they will faithfully review and look over the accounts. And the appointees have to listen to the parties if they should say that there is an error in the addition or things were omitted from the account; and if the error is proven and that error was large, the judge will retract the first account where it was incorrect. And if the error was small, the account having been examined, would not be reviewed.

And note that the verification of the accounts that the first and later *contadores* make does not have the force of a sentence so that it can be carried out.

But know that the *contadores* have to examine and verify the accounts, saying as follows: that they have verified the administrator having received so many thousand *maravedis* and having given and spent so many and have deducted the expenditures from the receipts the lord hands over to the administrator. And the *contadores* having made this investigation shall bring it before the judge and *escrivano* [scribe]; and they shall swear that they have examined and investigated the account well and loyally and they have not been able to find out anything else. And the judge with the accounts exhibited shall look them over attentively to see whether the *contadores* have overlooked something which could not justly be overlooked or if they omitted something which ought to be taken into account; and he shall order by sentence that the administrator pay the balance or the master pay if the administrator was shorted. Which is contrary to the opinion of many *contadores* and against other persons who are named to examine and verify accounts and to appraise houses, fortresses and other things. Who make their appraisal and having made it say that they are pronouncing it as a sentence and some judges who little know the law order that the sentence, given by the appraisers, be carried out and often these sentences and orders of execution amount to nothing because neither the appraisers nor the *contadores* have the power to sentence but only to appraise and verify; the judge has to sentence what is appraised and verified.

Note also that the verification made by *contadores* constituted by the judge makes full proof when they are set up between private individuals. But if it were made between public persons such as between the public treasury of the king and his *contadores* or between churches and their trustees and stewards, they do not constitute complete proof.

Finally note that the first accounts have to be reexamined, it having been proven that they were in error. This is true when the first accounts were examined unjustly by persons who had sufficient power to examine them because it would be as if the account had never been verified. In the same way, if the tutor or guardian should render account to their ward but the guardian should take account from the tutor without the authority of the judge, the ward would be able to seek restitution against such an account. But if it were rendered with the authority of the judge it could not be restored.

Part Eleven

As for the eleventh part in which we relate: if one of the parties says that there is an error in the account, how much time must elapse before a request that the account be reexamined for error can no longer be made. I say that if one of the parties asks that the account be withdrawn because of some slackness on the part of the *contadores*, as when the *contadores* permit the tutor or administrator some execution that they ought not to permit or they count what they should not, then the aggrieved party can request that the accounts be examined again within twenty years after the first accounts were made.

But if he asks that the account be withdrawn because it is in error, he can request that it be withdrawn up to 30 years. And those years having passed nothing can be requested against the account because the account has by the passage of time the force of a sentence.

And this applies not only to the administrator of the public treasury but also to any other administrator.

Part Twelve

As for the twelfth part in which we relate: how, after the account has been examined, payment of any outstanding balance has to be made. I say that if the balance consists of chattels or livestock, the administrator has to give his lord what remains and if it is real property he has to put him in possession of it.

But to my mind this may not be sufficient remedy for the lord to collect his goods except where the guardian or administrator hands them over voluntarily. But if he does not wish to give them, some want to say that the lord can seize the administrator and take him prisoner until he has paid if he is not also the administrator of someone else. Thus it is done in Salamanca and Zamora. And if the lord cannot seize him directly he can ask the judge to seize him or order him to be seized and taken prisoner until he pays up. The judge first ought to have had information regarding the debt and that suspicion exists against the administrator that he will flee. In this case there is no contract or sentence against the administrator but if there is an account verified by sentence or contract, the sentence or contract will be carried out. And if goods are not found on which they may execute, the administrator will be a prisoner until he pays or cedes the goods. And if the lord is a privileged person as is the public treasury, the church, certain wards or a university, he can collect his goods from the person to whom the administrator transferred them, requesting restitution in entirety.

On the other hand, if the lord owes the balance, the administrator can keep goods until he is paid. And if he has none of the master's goods he can ask that payment of the balance be carried out if it was sentenced according to what we said above regarding the lord against the administrator.

Part Thirteen

As for the thirteenth part in which we relate, if the administrator pays his master any outstanding balance and that having been done, goods are found in the administrator's possession or he has become rich: is he presumed to have badly managed or stolen the lord's goods, or earned them with his own goods elsewhere by his own industry. This question or dispute, upon which there are a variety of opinions, is continuous between lords and administrators.

One opinion regarding the officials of the public treasury and of the cities and other places: they are presumed to have earned by means of the office they held what they are found to possess after the term of office has expired. There is not this opportunity for those that held the administration of private goods. And they say that many tyrannical lords hold this opinion and seldom do their stewards leave their hands with any money because they firmly believe that the stewards acquired it with their goods; and this they affirm because they say that those things the official gains during the term of office he is presumed to have made in respect of the office.

And here they also say that if the official during his term of office bought something, he is presumed to have bought it with the goods of the office or charge he held.

And with the help of this presumption they say that the lord can ask and collect from the administrator all that the administrator bought or earned during the office. But if the administrator, against this presumption, wants to prove that he has the goods from elsewhere as by inheritance or a gift that was made to him or that he bought or earned in some other way; this proof will be sufficient to exclude the presumption against the administrator. They say that this presumption is sufficient for them to torture the administrator so that he declares from where he had the goods that are found in his possession once the charge he held has finished.

Others say that if this opinion were true it would be remarkable because it does not appear truthful to them. Rather they say the tutor is not presumed to have enriched himself with the ward's goods even though the tutor was poor at the time that he assumed the tutelage. Better proof is required to convict the tutor.

If the guardian or administrator procured the office, he is not presumed to have gained what he has with the office nor is he presumed to have hidden some of his master's goods unless it is proved. Because any man is presumed good if it has not been proved to the contrary. And they say that the first opinion bears on the prelates of churches and monasteries that administer the goods while they live. And if they don't distribute them in pious works what remains they hold back; he is seen to guard and reserve it for his church. And such a prelate neither by industry or work is presumed to have earned anything. But we talk about the administrator who gains for himself and not for another. And consequently what is said about the prelate of the church has no bearing on the officials of temporal lords. From which they conclude that his term of office having finished, the prelate is assumed to have derived all that he possesses from his office, dignity or prelature unless it is proved that he had it from an inheritance or gift, etc.

But the said presumption does not bear on another kind of administrator.

In truth, the question of the said proposition is doubtful according to the authority and reasoning of those who wrote about it. So that the issue is clear and correct under emendation of a better opinion, I agree with the opinion of others who wrote on this subject. I say that the *contadores*, the judges and other individuals who want to know the truth in this matter and to act as they ought, have to consider if the official or administrator is a person who can negotiate and understand the matters or dealings in which he stands to gain. If he is also an industrious person, they will presume that he earned what he has by his own industry and not with his master's goods, especially if he has goods of his own which he dealt in at the time that he took the charge. Then it is presumed that he earned what he has with his own goods and by his own industry.

But when the administrator is an individual who is prohibited from negotiating or dealing, the law presumes that he earned what he has with his master's goods or unjustly.

Thus I say that if the administrator renders a good account it is presumed that he committed no fraud involving the lord's goods, rather he earned what he has by his own industry.

On the other hand, if the administrator does not render a good account, he is presumed to have gained what he has with the lord's goods.

Likewise, if the administrator hid some things from among the goods that he administered and they were found, the account having been completed, it is understood that he had the intention of stealing them. And that the rest that he has has been gained with his master's goods.

Finally, this is a matter for the knowledge and discretion of the judge, the contrary notwithstanding. If there is strong suspicion against the administrator because he is a bad man and engaged in wrongful transactions or because they found he had hidden some of the master's goods or because he rendered a bad account; or if there is some presumption that favors the administrator, that he is a man of good repute or that he rendered a good account or that he is a man who has dealings or property of his own with which he can make a gain; then such presumptions as these exclude any other presumption regarding the administrator.

Here follows the fourteenth and final part of the present work.

Part Fourteen

As for the last and final part of this treatise in which we relate: if a copy of the accounts has to be rendered and how the written instrument has to be made; and the accounts, positions and sentence having been rendered, if the judge must execute the sentence even though it is appealed.

As for the first, I say that an authentic copy of the accounts has to be given to the lord and to other persons who have a legal interest in them.

And the instrument of the accounts has to be made in this manner. "On a certain day in such a month and year before me, the public notary, and witnesses written below, so-and-so; and so-and-so, *contadores*, retained by so-and-so and so-and-so in order to examine and verify their accounts. They examined them and verified them in the following manner." Here the notary will set down in writing the text of the accounts according to what was verified. And then at the foot of the accounts he will set down, "and thus the said *contadores* having examined and verified the said accounts, the parties being present or absent, they said that they found the accounts well rendered as far as they could tell with they information they had." And if the parties consented and approved them and considered them well rendered as well he will write it down and the *contadores* will sign the accounts or others will sign on their behalf if they know how to write. He then puts down the witnesses before whom it is pronounced. The parties will also sign this act. Since this act resembles a judgment or act of judgment, it has the force of a pact and it is necessary that it be signed according to the laws of these kingdoms.

The positions are set down in this manner on the master's part: "I put forward as a position that on a certain day in such a month and year, so-and-so took from me in administration such goods and each year that he had the said administration produced so many *maravedis* and so many measures of wheat."

The sentence has to be made in this manner: "Having seen the accounts rendered between so-and-so and so-and-so, I order that these observe and comply with the provisions contained in the sentence."

Regarding whether the sentence has to be executed: I say that it has to be carried out even though it is appealed. Proclamation of the goods having been made, execution is completed and payment of any balance will be made to the lord, the lord first having given security that he will pay double what he receives if in the second instance the sentence is revoked.

And if in the second instance the sentence is confirmed the lord will be paid and thus the account and dispute that the lord and administrator had will be finished.

{There is some doubt concerning this article. For example, one is condemned to render account to another for the goods that he or his father administered. The sentence was passed and the one in whose favor the sentence was given requests that it be executed so that the condemned is considered a debtor. It is doubtful if this sentence may be extended so that the condemned should pay what was verified in the account; some say that the sentence may not be extended to more than it calls for. But the truth is, such a sentence may be extended so that the one who was short in the account pays the other the balance because to render account is nothing but paying what is counted. Because it is also said that if a slave is bequeathed freedom on condition that he render account to the master's heir, by these words it is understood that he should give to the master's heir the instruments and other things that he held in administration. Thus to render account comprises two things: the first, to render account; the other, to restore what is owed. So that with the account verified between the master's heir and the administrator, execution can be requested and performed for the administrator's outstanding balance without other sentence or declaration.}

And this account is rendered of temporal goods to which all who administer the goods of others are obligated.

We are all generally obligated to give another kind of account of our works upon the coming of our Savior Jesus Christ on the Day of Judgment. Pray to Him that in this world we might do such works, that we may administer our life in such a way that we may render a good account and that we may deserve to hear that sweet voice. *Venite benedicti patris mei, etc. Amen.*

finis:

Laus immenso deo.

TABLE OF CONTENTS OF THE PRESENT WORK

Here begins the table of contents of the present work, in which the parts it consists of are found, arranged by their page numbers. Firstly,

The fourteenth and final part, which treats whether a copy of the accounts has to be given; and how the instrument with the accounts, positions and sentence has to be made.

END OF TABLE

Here ends the present work, the *Treatise on Accounts*, written by the *licenciado* Diego del Castillo, native of the city of Molina. It was printed in Salamanca by Juan de Junta book printer. It was finished on the 24th day of the month of July. The year 1[5]51.

ILLUSTRATIONS

¶ Tratado de cuẽtas
hecho por el licenciado Diego del
castillo: natural ð la ciudad de Mo
lina. En el qual se contiene que co-
sa es cuenta/ y a quiẽ/ y como han
de dar la cuenta los tutores y
otros administradores de
bienes agenos.
Obra muy necessaria y prouecho
sa: agora nueuamente addi-
cionada por el mesmo
autor.

1. Title page from the 1542 edition

dos marauedis/dizen que fueron tres:y eſtos ta
les deuen ſer punidos / en pena del doblo.[v] ¶ Y
por ellos ſe dize que muchos officiales y admini
ſtradores/ſon lobos robadores y perros de corte
que con diuerſas maneras y grandes aſtucias y
engaños: ſin que los ſienten deguellan las oue-
jas/ y ſe beuen la ſangre dellas:[x] Y avn digo por
lo que vi muchas vezes / que no ſe contentan cõ
la ſangre:mas tambien ſe comen la carne haſta
que llegan al hueſſo/y aquel ſe comeriã ſino fue-
ſſe tan duro:y tambien lo dexã penſando que ſo-
bre porna carne nueua/y ſe la tornaran a comer.
Y ſi algunos q̃ſieren penſar en todas partes po
dran hallar muchos adminiſtradores ricos q̃ de
ante ningunos bienes tenian/y yo los vi. Y a los
ſeñores pobres/ o muy alcançados y adeudados
tãbiẽ ſe dize q̃ eſtos tales adminiſtradores y rece
ptores/muchos males ſabẽ y cometẽ mas q̃ otros.[y]
Y es porq̃ los dineros ciegã los ojos d̃los admi-
niſtradores:codiciãdo hazer ſuyo el diero agẽo.[z]

Quanto a la octaua par-
te en que diximos en que coſas ſe dara
credito al libro delos adminiſtradores
y en que no/por que eſta parte es vna delas prin
cipales deſte tratado: hago della tres miẽbros.
¶ El primero es/o pregũtamos:ſi el libro de cuẽ
tas prueua en fauor de quien lo eſcriuio. ¶ O ſi
prueua contra quien lo eſcriuio. ¶ O cõtra otro
tercero. ¶ Quanto a lo primero ſi prueua en fa-
uor de quiẽ lo eſcriuio:algunos dizen que en las
coſas que dependen dela voluntad del q̃ lo eſcri-

Doblo.[v] ¶ Lex.j.§ ſuperxacto tribu.li.x.

Dellas.[x] ¶ Bar.in l.oẽs populi.x.coll̃.ꝟſi.circa primũ in fi. ff.de iuſti.ꝛ iure.

Otros.[y] ¶ In aut. vt indices ſine q̊quo ſufra.§.j.coll̃.ij.glo. in.l.facultas de iure fiſ.lib.x.et aut.de ex-hib.ꝛ intro.reis.§.j. coll̃.v.

Ageno.[z] ¶ Habet ecclesiaſtici.xx.in fi.

2. Folio from the 1552 edition showing the end of part seven

Fee. s. ¶ Lex.ij.C. de vsu. z. fructi. lega.

Ellas. t. ¶ Per dictam.l.j.C. de errore calculi.

Hiziera. v. ¶ Nã excedunt metas suc. iurisdictionis.l.fi.ff.de iu.omni iu.d.l.j.C.si a non cõpe.iudi.

Restituydo. u. ¶ Lex j.C.si aduer.solu.

Restituydo. x. ¶ Bal.in.di. le.j. quem vide.

res/o entre yglesias y sus sindicos z inconomos no hazen entera fee.[s] ¶ Finalmente es de notar q̃ las primeras cuentas se tienen de rehazer prouando se primero que interuino yerro en ellas:[t] Esto es verdad quando las cuentas primeras se hizieron injustamente por personas que tuuieron poder bastante para hazer las: porq̃ de otra manera seria la cuẽta como si nunca se hiziera:[v] Ansi como el tutor/o el curador diessen cuenta a su menor: mas si el curador tomasse cuenta al tutor sin auctoridad de juez: contra la tal cuẽta podria el menor pedir ser restituydo.[u]. Y si la diesse cõ auctoridad de juez/no podra ser restituydo.[x].

QUanto a la onzena parte en que diximos si vna dlas partes dixo q̃ vuo yerro en la cuenta: hasta quãto tiempo podra pedir q̃ se torne a hazer y se vea si vuo yerro en ella: digo que si vna delas partes pide que se retrate la cuẽta/ por razon de alguna gracia/o suelta q̃ los cõtadores hizieron en ella: ansi como si los contadores admittierõ al tutor/ o administrador alguna execucion que no deuieran admittir/o porque contauan en principio lo que contar no podian: estonce podra el agrauiado pedir que tornen a hazer las cuentas dentro de veynte años despues que las primeras cuentas se hizieron.[y]. ¶ Mas sino pide que se retrate la cuenta por esta razõ / saluo porque se herro en la cuenta: podra pedir que se retratẽ fasta treynta años.[z]. Y aquellos passados no se puede pedir cõtra ella cosa alguna: porque tiene ya la cuẽ

Hizieron. y. ¶ Intellige. sm distictionẽ possitã in.l. nominibus. §.j.ff.de diuer. z temp.prescri.

Años. z. ¶ L.calculi. ff.de admi. rer. ad ciui. pti.l.aduersus. C.de nego.gestis.vide hodie in.l.lxxij.legũ tauri.z bar.i.l.ij. de iure.fisci.lib.x.

3. The beginning of part eleven

ta por el trãſcurſo dſte tiẽpo fuerça de ſentẽcia.[z]. ¶ Y eſto a lugar no ſolamente enel adminiſtrador dl fiſco: mas en otro ꝗlꝗer adminiſtrador.[a].

Sẽtẽcia. ¶ Bar. i. d. l. ij. ff. ad aliqd ⁊ ibi glo. de. iure. fiſ. lib. x.

Adminiſtrador.[a]. ¶ Gloſa. in rub. d iure fiſ. lib. x. bar. i d. l. ij. ff. qro vtrum hec lex. de iure fiſci. lib. x.

QUanto a la dozena parte en que diximos que hecha la cuenta / ſe tiene de hazer pago del alcançe. Digo que ſi el alcançe es de coſa mueble / o ſemouiente: el adminiſtrador tiene de dar al ſeñor lo que ſobra: y ſi es rayz / lo tiene de poner en poſſeſſion della.[b]. ¶ Mas a mi ver eſte no es baſtante remedio para q el ſeñor cobre los bienes: ſaluo en caſo que el tutor / o adminiſtrador ſe los entrega de ſu voluntad: mas ſi no quiere dar los algunos quieren dezir que podra el ſeñor prender al adminiſtrador y tener lo preſo / haſta ſer pagado: ſi no es tambien adminiſtrador de otro y que anſi ſe vſa en Salamãca y çamora.[c]. Y que ſi no pudo el ſeñor prẽder lo / podra pedir al juez que lo prenda / o mande prender y tener preſo / haſta que ſea pagado: y el juez anſi lo deue hazer auida primero informacion dela deuda: y que aya ſoſpecha cõtra el adminiſtrador que ſe auſentara con ella.[d]. Eſto es anſi en caſo que no ay contrato ni ſentencia contra el adminiſtrador. mas ſi ay cuenta aueriguada por ſentencia / o contrato: ſera entregado el ſeñor por via de execuciõ.[e]. Y ſi no ſe hallan bienes en que lo executen: eſtara preſo el adminiſtrador haſta que pague / o haga ceſſion de bienes.[f]. Y ſi el ſeñor es perſona preuilegiada como es el fiſco: la ygleſia / algũ menor o vniuerſidad podra cobrar ſus bienes / dela per

Della.[b]. Bar. ꝯſilio ſuo qd incipit cicolꝰ

çamora.[c]. ¶ Refert ⁊ tenet. lex. ſtili. cxij.

Ella.[d]. ¶ Lex. lxvj. legũ tauri. iuncto. §. ſed hodie de ſatiſda inſti.

Execuciõ.[e]. ¶ Lex. iiij. ⁊. v. ti. delas ecceptiones. lib. ordi.

Bienes.[f]. ¶ Juxta formaz tex. i. l. j. ⁊ per totũ. C. q. bo. ce. po. l. v. t. dlas deudas in ordi. meliꝰ i pragma. fo. xcv. cũ tribꝰ ſeqn.

4. Continuation of part eleven

Tabla dela presente obra.

¶ Comiença la tabla dela presente obra: en la qual se hallaran las partes que en ella se contienen ordenadamēte por el numero de sus hojas. Primeramente.

5. The table of contents to the 1552 edition

Fin dela tabla.

¶ Aqui ſe da fin a la preſente obra y tratado de cuentas / hecho por el licenciado Diego dl caſtillo: natural dla cibdad de Molina. Cō priuilegio Real que ninguno lo pueda vender ni imprimir en eſtos reynos: ſaluo la perſona / o perſonas que ſu poder ouierē / por eſpacio de diez años: ſegun que por la cedula y priuilegio de ſus Mageſtades pareſce. Es impreſſo en la muy noble y mas leal cibdad de Burgos por Alonſo de Melgar. Acaboſe a. xxx. dias del mes de Mayo / Año de mill y. D. y. xxij. años.

6. Continuation of the table of contents

7. Colophon from the 1522 edition

NOTES AND REFERENCES

NOTES TO THE TRANSLATION

Introduction

1. In the United States, Columbia University Library, New York; Folger Shakespeare Library, Washington, D.C.; and the collections of the Hispanic Society of America, New York. In the United Kingdom, the British Library. In Spain, Biblioteca Nacional, Madrid; Biblioteca de Palacio, Madrid; Universidad de Oviedo; Universidad de Salamanca.

2. The remaining material in this essay is reprinted in part from *The Accounting Historians Journal*, vol. 13, no. 2, Fall 1986, pp.65-76 and vol. 14, no. 1, Spring 1987, pp. 95-108 with permission of The Academy of Accounting Historians. Some additional material has been added.

3. For a concise description of this early literature, see Hernández Esteve [1985b, pp. 291-92].

4. See Gonzalez Ferrando [pp. 36-54] for a thorough discussion of what is known concerning Del Castillo's life and writings. The biographical material related here is derived from his essay.

5. Hernández Esteve [1981, pp. 102-123] lists these writers and provides information concerning their backgrounds, works and influence.

6. Del Castillo cites several other authors whose works and identities have proved impossible to trace. They are: Andreas de Isarnia; Johannes de Platea; Nicolaus de Neapo; and Petrus Girardi.

7. Jouanique [1983, p. 338] encountered similar difficulties in interpreting the terminology in the acts of the Genoese *Rota*.

8. For a complete exposition of the hierarchy of proofs in Roman law procedure, see Levy [1939].

Prologue

1. Charles I, first Habsburg king of Spain, ruled from 1517 until his abdication in 1556; in 1519 he also became Holy Roman Emperor and reigned as Charles V until his death in 1558.

2. The *curador* or guardian was appointed to caretake the goods and business affairs of a minor; the *tutor* was primarily responsible for the education and care of a minor but incidentally might also administer the minor's goods.

3. Indicating the holder of a higher degree in law above the baccalaureate.

4. The town Molina de Aragon in the province of Guadalajara.

5. As was the practice in legal, indeed, in all scholarly literature of the day, Del Castillo provided citations to the most authoritative sources to support his arguments. These citations comprise the gloss of the work and appear, as Del Castillo states, in the margins of the text. A translation of the gloss has not been provided in the present work, principally because these notes are not relevant to the understanding of the text. The Introduction gives some of the authors and texts cited.

Hernández Esteve [1981, pp. 102-20] gives the authors most cited by Muñoz de Escobar and Hevia Bolaño in the accounting portions of their treatises. Jouanique [1966b, pp. 42-50] provides a similar listing for Muñoz de Escobar.

6. Del Castillo considered these words synonyms; in Part One he explains that "at law there is no difference between *cuenta* or *razon*." The closest English equivalent of both is "account."

7. The instrument, positions, and sentence were actual documents representing stages in a suit conducted according to civil law procedure.

Part One

1. For further discussion of Del Castillo's three forms of keeping accounts, see the Introduction.

Part Two

1. Part of the special status accorded clerics beginning in the fourth century. *Privilegium canonis* provided that any person who struck a cleric was subject to excommunication. It was also forbidden to summon a clerk before a lay court of justice although Del Castillo apparently disputes this view.

2. In the Middle Ages, a family firm; later it admitted foreign partners and accepted money from depositors. All partners, who contributed capital, labor or both, were jointly liable. For a concise history of the firm from the fifteenth to the eighteenth centuries, see Braudel [1979, pp. 434-57].

3. In such a case, the father released a minor son from *patria potestas*, thus giving the child the right to administer his own goods without the intervention of tutor or guardian.

4. Derived from Roman law, the right to use and profit from property belonging to another as long as the property was not damaged or altered.

5. Originally, the private property of a son acquired by military service.

Part Three

1. The administrator would be indebted to his principal for the balance (*el alcance*) of the account if the sum of "*el rescibo*" surpassed that of "*la data.*" Please see the Introduction for further discussion of agential bookkeeping.

2. The money of account in Castile during the sixteenth and seventeenth centuries.

3. Known in some Spanish cities as *assistente*, the *corregidor* was the representative of royal authority in the town and president *ex officio* of the municipal council.

4. Municipal councilmen; also known as *los veinticuatros* after the standard number (24) of such offices in town government although the number varied.

5. Conciliar officials who represented and defended the interests of the town's inhabitants.

6. One of the first documents introduced in a civil law suit, summarizing the allegations on which the action was based and requesting a specific judgment by the court.

7. *Acta judicialia*; the recorded proceedings of a suit.

Part Four

1. An inventory of the goods and property committed to the administrator's care was commonly the first entry.

Part Five

1. Derived from the Roman law, a contract granting long-term or perpetual possession of agricultural land subject to certain conditions, such as keeping the land cultivated or paying an annual rent.

2. Rent on the possession and cultivation of agricultural land; a type of manorial dues.

3. Possibly the *Glossa Ordinaria* of Accursius, the thirteenth-century compilation of commentary on the *Corpus iuris civilis.*

4. Prince Charles, later Charles I of Spain and Holy Roman Emperor, to whom Del Castillo dedicated his tract, inherited the Low Countries, including Flanders, from his father Philip of Burgundy in 1506.

Part Seven

1. A type of royal tax voted by the Cortes of Castile and imposed on all the subjects of the realm, including vassals.

2. The *alcabala* was a tax on sales; *tercias reales* a clerical tax. In the early sixteenth century, it became common practice for the towns to pay a fixed sum, called the *encabezamiento*, in lieu of the full value of the *alcabala.*

3. The Catholic Kings, Ferdinand II of Aragon (+1516) and Isabella I of Castile (+1504).

Part Eight

1. Formal judgment of the court.

Part Nine

1. A member of the lesser aristocracy in Castile; also called *hidalgo.*

2. As a perpetual right; normally used of rights to regular money payments or pensions.

Part Ten

1. Feudal homage, the relationship between feudal lord and his vassal.

REFERENCES

Braudel, F., *The Wheels of Commerce (Civilization and Capitalism, 15th-18th Centuries)* (Harper & Row, 1979).

Elliott, J.H. *Imperial Spain, 1469-1716* (St. Martin's Press, 1963).

Gonzalez Ferrando, J.M., "De las tres formas de llevar 'cuenta y razon' segun el licenciado Diego del Castillo, natural de Molina" (unpublished paper).

Hernández Esteve, E., Fernandez Pena, E., Prado Caballero, J.M., and Esteo Sanchez, F., *Spanish Accounting in the Past and Present* (Strathclyde Convergencies, 1981).

Hernández Esteve, E., *Contribución al estudio de la historiografia contable en España* (Banco de España, 1981).

__________________, "Tras las huellas de Bartolomé Salvador de Solórzano, autor del primer tratado español de contabilidad por partida doble," *Revista de derecho mercantil* (1983), pp. 125-66.

__________________, "Las cuentas de Fernan Lopez del Campo, primer factor general de Felipe II para los reinos de España (1556-1560)," *Hacienda Publica Española* (1984), pp. 85-105.

__________________, "Legislación castellana de la baja Edad Media y comienzos del Renacimiento sobre contabilidad y libros de cuentas de mercaderes," *Hacienda Publica Española* (1985a) pp. 197-221.

__________________, "A Spanish Treatise of 1706 on Double-Entry Bookkeeping: 'Norte Mercantil y Crisol de Cuentas' by Gabriel de Souza Brito," *Accounting and Business Research* (Autumn 1985b), pp. 291-96.

Jouanique, P., "La comptabilité dans les decisions de la Rote de Genes (1528-1582)," *Proceedings, Quarto Congresso Internazionale di Storia della Ragioneria* (Pisa, 1984), pp. 329-48.

____________________, "La vie et l'oeuvre de Francisco Muñoz de Escobar," *Revue belge de la comptabilité* (no. 3, 1965a), pp. 11-26; (no. 4, 1965b), pp. 59-67; (no. 1, 1966a), pp. 39-49; (no. 2, 1966b), pp. 35-50.

Kagan, R.L., *Lawsuits and Litigants in Castile, 1500-1700* (University of North Carolina Press, 1981)

Lea, H.C., *The Duel and the Oath* (University of Pennsylvania Press, 1974).

Levy, J.Ph., *La hierarchie des preuves dans le droit savant du moyen-âge depuis la Renaissance du Droit Romain jusqu'à la fin de XIVe siècle* (Annales de l'Université de Lyon, 1939).

Lynch, J., *Spain Under the Habsburgs* (Oxford University Press, 1964).

Mills, P.A., "Financial Reporting and Stewardship Accounting in Sixteenth-Century Spain," *Accounting Historians Journal* (Fall 1986), pp. 65-76.

____________________, "The Probative Capacity of Accounts in Early-Modern Spain," *Accounting Historians Journal* (Spring 1987), pp. 95-108.

Accounting Books Published by Garland

NEW BOOKS

■ *Altman, Edward I., *The Prediction of Corporate Bankruptcy: A Discriminant Analysis.*
New York, 1988.

■ Ashton, Robert H., ed. *The Evolution of Accounting Behavior Research: An Overview.*
New York, 1984.

■ Ashton, Robert H., ed. *Some Early Contributions to the Study of Audit Judgement.*
New York, 1984.

■ *Bodenhorn, Diran. *Economic Accounting.*
New York, 1988.

---

* Included in the Garland series Foundations of Accounting
† Included in the Academy of Accounting Historians, Classics Series, Gary John Previt, ed.

■ *Bougen, Philip D. *Accounting and Industrial Relations: Some Historical Evidence on Their Interaction.*
New York, 1988.

■ Brief, Richard P., ed. *Corporate Financial Reporting and Analysis in the Early 1900s.*
New York, 1986.

■ Brief, Richard P., ed. *Depreciation and Capital Maintenance.*
New York, 1984.

■ Brief, Richard P., ed. *Estimating the Economic Rate of Return from Accounting Data.*
New York, 1986.

■ Brief, Richard P., ed. *Four Classics on the Theory of Double-Entry Bookkeeping.*
New York, 1982.

■ Chambers, R. J., and G. W. Dean, eds. *Chambers on Accounting.*
New York, 1986.

Volume I: Accounting, Management and Finance.
Volume II: Accounting Practice and Education.
Volume III: Accounting Theory and Research.
Volume IV: Price Variation Accounting.
Volume V: Continuously Contemporary Accounting.

■ *Clark, John B. (with a new introduction by Donald Dewey). *Capital and Its Earnings.*
New York, 1988.

- Clarke, F. L. *The Tangled Web of Price Variation Accounting: The Development of Ideas Underlying Professional Prescriptions in Six Countries.*
  New York, 1982.

- Coopers & Lybrand. *The Early History of Coopers & Lybrand.*
  New York, 1984.

- Craswell, Allen. *Audit Qualifications in Australia 1950 to 1979.*
  New York, 1986.

- Dean, G. W., and M. C. Wells, eds. *The Case for Continuously Contemporary Accounting.*
  New York, 1984.

- Dean, G. W. , and M. C. Wells, eds. *Forerunners of Realizable Values Accounting in Financial Reporting.*
  New York, 1982.

- Edey, Harold C. *Accounting Queries.*
  New York, 1982.

- Edwards, J. R., ed. *Legal Regulation of British Company Accounts 1836-1900.*
  New York, 1986.

- Edwards, J. R. ed. *Reporting Fixed Assets in Nineteenth-Century Company Accounts.*
  New York, 1986.

- Edwards, J. R., ed. *Studies of Company Records: 1830-1974.*
  New York, 1984.

■ Fabricant, Solomon. *Studies in Social and Private Accounting.*
New York, 1982.

■ Gaffikin, Michael, and Michael Aitkin, eds. *The Development of Accounting Theory: Significant Contributors to Accounting Thought in the 20th Century.*
New York, 1982.

■ Hawawini, Gabriel A., ed. *Bond Duration and Immunization: Early Developments and Recent Contributions.*
New York, 1982.

■ Hawawini, Gabriel A., and Pierre A. Michel, eds. *European Equity Markets: Risk, Return, and Efficiency.*
New York, 1984.

■ Hawawini, Gabriel A., and Pierre Michel. *Mandatory Financial Information and Capital Market Equilibrium in Belgium.*
New York, 1986.

■ Hawkins, David F. *Corporate Financial Disclosure, 1900-1933: A Study of Management Inertia within a Rapidly Changing Environment.*
New York, 1986.

■ *Hopwood, Anthony G. *Accounting from the Outside: The Collected Papers of Anthony G. Hopwood.*
New York, 1988.

■ Johnson, H. Thomas. *A New Approach to Management Accounting History.*
New York, 1986.

■ Kinney, William R., ed. *Fifty Years of Statistical Auditing.*
New York, 1986.

■ Klemstine, Charles E., and Michael W. Maher. *Management Accounting Research: A Review and Annotated Bibliography.*
New York, 1984.

■ *Langenderfer, Harold Q., and Grover L. Porter, eds. *Rational Accounting Concepts: The Writings of Willard Graham.*
New York, 1988.

■ *Lee, T. A., ed. *The Evolution of Audit Thought and Practice.*
New York, 1988.

■ Lee, T. A., ed. *A Scottish Contribution to Accounting History.*
New York, 1986.

■ Lee, T. A. *Towards a Theory and Practice of Cash Flow Accounting.*
New York, 1986.

■ Lee, T. A., ed. *Transactions of the Chartered Accountants Students' Societies of Edinburgh and Glasgow: A Selection of Writings, 1886-1958.*
New York, 1984.

■ *Loft, Anne. *Understanding Accounting in Its Social and Historical Context: The Case of Cost Accounting in Britain, 1914-1925.*
New York, 1988.

■ McKinnon, Jill L.. *The Historical Development and Operational Form of Corporate Reporting Regulation in Japan.*
New York, 1986.

■ *McMickle, Peter L., and Paul H. Jensen, eds. *The Auditor's Guide of 1869: A Review and Computer Enhancement of Recently Discovered Old Microfilm of America's First Book on Auditing by H. J. Mettenheimer.*
New York, 1988.

■ *McMickle, Peter L., and Paul H. Jensen, eds. *The Birth of American Accountancy: A Bibliographic Analysis of Works on Accounting Published in America through 1820.*
New York, 1988.

■ *Mepham, M.-J. *Accounting in Eighteenth-Century Scotland.*
New York, 1988.

■ *Mills, Patti A., trans. *The Legal Literature of Accounting: On Accounts by Diego del Castillo.*
New York, 1988.

■ *Murphy, George J. *The Evolution of Canadian Corporate Reporting Practices: 1900-1970.*
New York, 1988.

■ *Mumford, Michael J., ed. *Edward Stamp—Later Papers.*
New York, 1988.

■ Nobes, Christopher, ed. *The Development of Double Entry: Selected Essays.*
New York, 1984.

■ Nobes, Christopher. *Issues in International Accounting.*
New York, 1986.

■ Parker, Lee D. *Developing Control Concepts in the 20th Century.*
New York, 1986.

■ *Parker, Lee D., ed. *Financial Reporting to Employees: From Past to Present.*
New York, 1988.

■ *Parker, Lee D., and O. Finley Graves, eds. *Methodology and Method in History: A Bibliography.*
New York, 1988.

■ Parker, R. H. *Papers on Accounting History.*
New York, 1984.

■ Previts, Gary John, and Alfred R. Roberts, eds. *Federal Securities Law and Accounting 1933-1970: Selected Addresses.*
New York, 1986.

■ *Reid, Jean Margo, ed. *Law and Accounting: Nineteenth-Century American Legal Cases.*
New York, 1988.

■ *Sheldahl, Terry K., ed. *Accounting Literature in the United States before Mitchell and Jones (1796): Contributions by Four English Writers, through American Editions, and Two Pioneer Local Authors.*
New York, 1988.

■ Sheldahl, Terry K. *Beta Alpha Psi, from Alpha to Omega: Pursuing a Vision of Professional Education for Accountants, 1919-1945.*
New York, 1982.

■ Sheldahl, Terry K. *Beta Alpha Psi, from Omega to Zeta Omega: The Making of a Comprehensive Accounting Fraternity, 1946-1984.*
New York, 1986.

■ *Sheldahl, Terry K., ed. *Education for the Mercantile Countinghouse: Critical and Constructive Essays by Nine British Writers, 1716-1794.*
New York, 1988.

■ Solomons, David. *Collected Papers on Accounting and Accounting Education (in two volumes).*
New York, 1984.

■ Sprague, Charles F. *The General Principles of the Science of Accounts and the Accountancy of Investment.*
New York, 1984.

■ Stamp, Edward. *Edward Stamp—Later Papers.* *See* Michael J. Mumford.

■ Stamp, Edward. *Selected Papers on Accounting, Auditing, and Professional Problems.*
New York, 1984.

■ *Staubus, George J. *Activity Costing for Decisions: Cost Accounting in the Decision Usefulness Framework.*
New York, 1988.

■ Storrar, Colin, ed. *The Accountant's Magazine—An Anthology.*
New York, 1986.

■ Tantral, Panadda. *Accounting Literature in Non-Accounting Journals: An Annotated Bibliography.*
New York, 1984.

■ *Vangermeersch, Richard G. *Alexander Hamilton Church: A Man of Ideas for All Seasons.*
New York, 1988.

■ Vangermeersch, Richard, ed. *The Contributions of Alexander Hamilton Church to Accounting and Management.*
New York, 1986.

■ Vangermeersch, Richard, ed. *Financial Accounting Milestones in the Annual Reports of the United States Steel Corporation—The First Seven Decades.*
New York, 1986.

■ *Walker, Stephen P. *The Society of Accountants in Edinburgh, 1854-1914: A Study of Recruitment to a New Profession.*
New York, 1988.

■ Whitmore, John. *Factory Accounts.*
New York, 1984.

■ *Whittred, Greg. *The Evolution of Consolidated Financial Reporting in Australia: An Evaluation of an Alternative Hypothesis.*
New York, 1988.

REPRINTED TITLES

- *American Institute of Accountants. *Accountants Index, 1920* (in two volumes).
  New York, 1921 (Garland reprint, 1988).

- American Institute of Accountants. *Fiftieth Anniversary Celebration.*
  Chicago, 1937 (Garland reprint, 1982).

- American Institute of Accountants. *Library Catalogue.*
  New York, 1919 (Garland reprint, 1982).

- Arthur Andersen Company. *The First Fifty Years 1913-1963.*
  Chicago, 1963 (Garland reprint, 1984).

- Bevis, Herman W. *Corporate Financial Reporting in a Competitive Economy.*
  New York, 1965 (Garland reprint, 1986).

- Bonini,. Charles P., Robert K. Jaedicke, and Harvey M. Wagner, eds. *Management Controls: New Directions in Basic Research.*
  New York, 1964 (Garland reprint, 1986).

- **The Book-Keeper and the American Counting Room.*
  New York, 1880-1884 (Garland reprint, 1988).

- Yamey, Basil S. *Further Essays on the History of Accounting.*
  New York, 1982.

- Zeff, Stephen A., ed. *The Accounting Postulates and Principles Controversy of the 1960s.*
  New York, 1982.

- Zeff, Stephen A., ed. *Accounting Principles Through the Years: The Views of Professional and Academic Leaders 1938-1954.*
  New York, 1982.

- Zeff, Stephen A., and Maurice Moonitz, eds. *Sourcebook on Accounting Principles and Auditing Procedures: 1917-1953 (in two volumes).*
  New York, 1984.

- *Zeff, Stephen a., ed. *The U. S. Accounting Profession in the 1890s and Early 1900s.*
  New York, 1988.

■ Bray, F. Sewell. *Four Essays in Accounting Theory.* London, 1953. *Bound with* Institute of Chartered Accountants in England and Wales and the National Institute of Economic and Social Research. *Some Accounting Terms and Concepts.*
Cambridge, 1951 (Garland reprint, 1982).

■ Brown, R. Gene, and Kenneth S. Johnston. *Paciolo on Accounting.*
New York, 1963 (Garland reprint, 1984).

■ Carey, John L., and William O. Doherty, eds. *Ethical Standards of the Accounting Profession.*
New York, 1966 (Garland reprint, 1986).

■ Chambers, R. J. *Accounting in Disarray.*
Melbourne, 1973 (Garland reprint, 1982).

■ Cooper, Ernest. *Fifty-seven years in an Accountant's Office.* *See* Sir Russell Kettle.

■ Couchman, Charles B. *The Balance-Sheet.*
New York, 1924 (Garland reprint, 1982).

■ Couper, Charles Tennant. *Report of the Trial ... Against the Directors and Manager of the City of Glasgow Bank.*
Edinburgh, 1879 (Garland reprint, 1984).

■ Cutforth, Arthur E. *Audits.*
London, 1906 (Garland reprint, 1982).

■ Cutforth, Arthur E. *Methods of Amalgamation.*
London, 1926 (Garland reprint, 1982).

■ Deinzer, Harvey T. *Development of Accounting Thought.*
New York, 1965 (Garland reprint, 1984).

■ De Paula, F.R.M. *The Principles of Auditing.*
London, 1915 (Garland reprint, 1984).

■ Dickerson, R. W. *Accountants and the Law of Negligence.*
Toronto, 1966 (Garland reprint, 1982).

■ Dodson, James. *The Accountant, or, the Method of Bookkeeping Deduced from Clear Principles, and Illustrated by a Variety of Examples.*
London, 1750 (Garland reprint, 1984).

■ Dyer, S. *A Common Sense Method of Double Entry Bookkeeping, on First Principles, as Suggested by De Morgan. Part I, Theoretical.*
London, 1897 (Garland reprint, 1984).

■ *† Edwards, James Don. *History of Public Accounting in the United States.*
East Lansing, 1960 (Garland reprint, 1988).

■ *† Edwards, James Don, and Robert F. Salmonson. *Contributions of Four Accounting Pioneers: Kohler, Littleton, May, Paton.*
East Lancing, 1961 (Garland reprint, 1988).

■ *The Fifth International Congress on Accounting, 1938 [Kongress-Archiv 1938 des V. Internationalen Prüfungs- und Treuhand-Kongresses].*
Berlin, 1938 (Garland reprint, 1986).

■ Finney, A. H. *Consolidated Statements.*
New York, 1922 (Garland reprint, 1982).

■ Fisher, Irving. *The Rate of Interest.*
New York, 1907 (Garland reprint, 1982).

■ Florence, P. Sargant. *Economics of Fatigue and Unrest and the Efficiency of Labour in English and American Industry.*
London, 1923 (Garland reprint, 1984).

■ *Fourth International Congress on Accounting 1933.*
London, 1933 (Garland reprint, 1982).

■ Foye, Arthur B. *Haskins & Sells: Our First Seventy-Five Years.*
New York, 1970 (Garland reprint, 1984).

■ *† Garner, Paul S. *Evolution of Cost Accounting to 1925.*
University, Alabama, 1925 (Garland reprint, 1988).

■ Garnsey, Sir Gilbert. *Holding Companies and Their Published Accounts.* London, 1923. *Bound with* Sir Gilbert Garnsey. *Limitations of a Balance Sheet.*
London, 1928 (Garland reprint, 1982).

■ Garrett, A. A. *The History of the Society of Incorporated Accountants, 1885-1957.*
Oxford, 1961 (Garland reprint, 1984).

■ Gilman, Stephen. *Accounting Concepts of Profit.*
New York, 1939 (Garland reprint, 1982).

■ Gordon, William. *The Universal Accountant, and Complete Merchant* ... [Volume II].
Edinburgh, 1765 (Garland reprint, 1986).

■ Green, Wilmer. *History and Survey of Accountancy.*
Brooklyn, 1930 (Garland reprint, 1986).

■ Hamilton, Robert. *An Introduction to Merchandise, Parts IV and V (Italian Bookkeeping and Practical Bookkeeping).*
Edinburgh, 1788 (Garland reprint, 1982).

■ Hatton, Edward. *The Merchant's Magazine; or, Tradesman's Treasury.* London, 1695 (Garland reprint, 1982).
Hills, George S. *The Law of Accounting and Financial Statements.*
Boston, 1957 (Garland reprint, 1982).

■ *A History of Cooper Brothers & Co. 1854 to 1954.*
London, 1954 (Garland reprint, 1986).

■ Hofstede, Geert. *The Game of Budget Control.*
Assen, 1967 (Garland reprint, 1984).

■ Howitt, Sir Harold. *The History of the Institute of Chartered Accountants in England and Wales 1880-1965, and of Its Founder Accountancy Bodies 1870-1880.*
London, 1966 (Garland reprint, 1984).

■ Institute of Chartered Accountants in England and Wales and The National Institute of Social and Economic Research. *Some Accounting Terms and Concepts. See* F. Sewell Bray.

■ Institute of Chartered Accountants of Scotland. *History of the Chartered Accountants of Scotland from the Earliest Times to 1954.*
Edinburgh, 1954 (Garland reprint, 1984).

■ *International Congress on Accounting 1929.*
New York, 1930 (Garland reprint, 1982).

■ Jaedicke, Robert K., Yuji Ijiri, and Oswald Nielsen, eds. *Research in Accounting Measurement.*
American Accounting Association,
1966 (Garland reprint, 1986).

■ Keats, Charles. *Magnificent Masquerade.*
New York, 1964 (Garland reprint, 1982).

■ Kettle, Sir Russell. *Deloitte & Co. 1854-1956.* Oxford, 1958. *Bound with* Ernest Cooper. *Fifty-seven Years in an Accountant's Office.*
London, 1921 (Garland reprint, 1982).

■ Kitchen, J., and R. H. Parker. *Accounting Thought and Education: Six English Pioneers.*
London, 1980 (Garland reprint, 1984).

■ Lacey, Kenneth. *Profit Measurement and Price Changes.*
London, 1952 (Garland reprint, 1982).

■ Lee, Chauncey. *The American Accomptant.*
Lansingburgh, 1797 (Garland reprint, 1982).

■ Lee, T. A., and R. H. Parker. *The Evolution of Corporate Financial Reporting.*
Middlesex, 1979 (Garland reprint, 1984).

[redacted]

■ *† Littleton, A. C.. *Accounting Evolution to 1900.*
New York, 1933 (Garland reprint, 1988).

■ Malcolm, Alexander. *The Treatise of Book-Keeping, or, Merchants Accounts; In the Italian Method of Debtor and Creditor; Wherein the Fundamental Principles of That Curious and Approved Method Are Clearly and Fully Explained and Demonstrated ... To Which Are Added, Instructions for Gentlemen of Land Estates, and Their Stewards or Factors: With Directions Also for Retailers, and Other More Private Persons.*
London, 1731 (Garland reprint, 1986).

■ Meij, J. L., ed. *Depreciation and Replacement Policy.*
Chicago, 1961 (Garland reprint, 1986).

■ Newlove, George Hills. *Consolidated Balance Sheets.*
New York, 1926 (Garland reprint, 1982).

■ North, Roger. *The Gentleman Accomptant; or, An Essay to Unfold the Mystery of Accompts; By Way of Debtor and Creditor, Commonly Called Merchants Accompts, and Applying the Same to the Concerns of the Nobility and Gentry of England.*
London 1714 (Garland reprint, 1986).

■ **Proceedings of the Seventh International Congress of Accountants.* Amsterdam, 1957 (Garland reprint, 1988).

■ Pryce-Jones, Janet E., and R. H. Parker. *Accounting in Scotland: A Historical Bibliography.*
Edinburgh, 1976 (Garland reprint, 1984).

[redacted]

■ *Reynolds, W. B., and F. W. Thornton. *Duties of a Junior Accountant* [three editions].
New York, 1917, 1933, 1953
(Garland reprint, 1988).

■ Robinson, H. W. *A History of Accountants in Ireland.*
Dublin, 1964 (Garland edition, 1984).

■ Robson, T. B. *Consolidated and Other Group Accounts.*
London, 1950 (Garland reprint, 1982).

■ Rorem, C. Rufus. *Accounting Method.*
Chicago, 1928 (Garland reprint, 1982).

■ Saliers, Earl A., ed. *Accountants' Handbook.*
New York, 1923 (Garland reprint, 1986).

■ Samuel, Horace B. *Shareholder's Money.*
London, 1933 (Garland reprint, 1982).

■ *The Securitites and Exchange Commission in the Matter of McKesson & Robbins, Inc. Report on Investigation.*
Washington, D. C., 1940 (Garland reprint, 1982).

■ *The Securities and Exchange Commission in the Matter of McKesson & Robbins, Inc. Testimony of Expert Witnesses.*
Washington, D. C., 1939 (Garland reprint, 1982).

■ Shaplen, Roger. *Kreuger: Genius and Swindler.*
New York, 1960 (Garland reprint, 1986).

■ Singer, H. W. *Standardized Accountancy in Germany. (With a new appendix.)*
Cambridge, 1943 (Garland reprint, 1982).

- *The Sixth International Congress on Accounting.*
  London, 1952 (Garland reprint, 1984).

- Stewart, Jas. C. (with a new introductory note by T. A. Lee). *Pioneers of a Profession: Chartered Accountants to 1879.*
  Edinburgh, 1977 (Garland reprint, 1986).

- Thompson, Wardbaugh. *The Accomptant's Oracle: or, a Key to Science, Being a Compleat Practical System of Book-keeping.*
  York, 1777 (Garland reprint, 1984).

- *Thornton, F. W. *Duties of the Senior Accountant.* New York, 1932. *Bound with.* John C. Martin. *Duties of Junior and Senior Accountants, Supplement of the CPA Handbook.*
  New York, 1953 (Garland reprint, 1988).

- Vatter, William J. *Managerial Accounting.*
  New York, 1950 (Garland reprint, 1986).

- Woolf, Arthur H. *A Short History of Accountants and Accountancy.*
  London, 1912 (Garland reprint, 1986).

- Yamey, B. S., H. C. Edey, and Hugh W. Thomson. *Accounting in England and Scotland: 1543-1800.*
  London, 1963 (Garland reprint, 1982).